SPATIAL PROBLEM SOLVING

WITH
PAPER FOLDING AND CUTTING

by

Patricia S. Davidson

Robert E. Willcutt

Cuisenaire Company of America, Inc.
12 Church Street, P.O. Box D
New Rochelle, New York 10802

A Special Note to Teachers

This workbook has been written with the intention of meeting some of the curricular needs uncovered by recent neurological research, specifically the need to make a more conscious effort to strengthen right hemispheric skills and to integrate left and right hemispheric thinking. Neurological research indicates that the two sides of the brain perform distinct functions; the left hemisphere being critical to verbal, logical, and sequential processing; and the right hemisphere specializing in spatial, perceptual, and holistic processing. It has been asserted that our culture and especially our school systems have overly stressed left hemispheric skills, often to the detriment of people's spatial reasoning experiences.

As a companion to **Spatial Problem Solving with Cuisenaire Rods**, which utilizes the concrete-to-pictorial modes, this work provides a pictorial-to-abstract development of spatial problem solving using the context of paper folding and paper cutting. This workbook has four major sections, starting with problems involving one fold, then two folds, and three folds, and then moving to challenging problems with added components, namely more than one possible type of fold and changes in orientation of the designs due to rotation and/or reflection.

Each section presents the problems in two styles of reasoning (whole-to-parts and parts-to-whole) in an attempt to provide integration between the styles of processing of the two hemispheres. The whole-to-parts problems encourage spatial, holistic processing; whereas the parts-to-whole problems require more detailed, step-by-step analytical reasoning along with spatial reasoning. Some students may find one type of thinking easier than the other. For some, the internal details in the parts-to-whole problems will be confusing distractions; while other students will latch onto them as important salient features helpful to the decision making process. The final section should be done only by students who have experienced the earlier sections with a great deal of success.

The activities can be done individually, in pairs, in small groups, or with a whole class. Students should be encouraged to compare and discuss their answers and problem solving strategies. Teaching suggestions and answers are given on pages 54 to 62.

Even though this workbook is intended for students in Grades 4 - 8, older students and adults of all ages will also benefit from these challenges to their spatial prowess.

TABLE OF CONTENTS

ONE FOLD LINE
Whole-to-Parts Relationships
Finding a Line of Symmetry 1, 2
Making Designs with Vertical Folds 3
Making Designs with Horizontal Folds 4
Matching a Given Design and its Folded Piece 5, 6
Matching Designs and Folded Pieces 7, 8
Finding Possible Folded Pieces for a Given Design 9, 10

Parts-to-Whole Relationships
Unfolding a Cut-out Piece 11, 12
Matching Cut-outs and Unfolded Pieces 13, 14
Finding the Unfolded Piece 15, 16
Drawing Unfolded Designs 17, 18
Matching Pairs for the Same Unfolded Design 19, 20

TWO FOLD LINES
Whole-to-Parts Relationships
Finding Two Lines of Symmetry 21
Finding Lines of Symmetry 22
Making Designs Using Two Lines of Symmetry 23
Matching a Given Design and its Doubly Folded Piece 24, 25
Finding Possible Folded Pieces for a Given Design 26
Matching Designs and Doubly Folded Pieces 27, 28
Finding Possible Folded Pieces for a Given Design 29, 30

Parts-to-Whole Relationships
Unfolding a Cut-out Piece 31, 32
Matching Cut-outs and Unfolded Pieces 33, 34
Finding the Unfolded Piece 35, 36
Drawing Unfolded Designs 37, 38
Matching Pairs for the Same Unfolded Design 39, 40

THREE FOLD LINES
Whole-to-Parts Relationships
Using Three Fold Lines 41
Matching Cut-outs and Unfolded Pieces 42
Matching a Given Design and its Triply Folded Piece 43
Finding Possible Triply Folded Pieces for a Given Design 44

Parts-to-Whole Relationships
Finding the Unfolded Piece 45, 46
Drawing Unfolded Designs 47, 48

CHANGES IN ORIENTATION
Whole-to-Parts Relationships
Rotating and Reflecting Pieces 49
Matching Designs with Rotated and Reflected Pieces 50

Parts-to-Whole Relationships
Matching Cut-outs and Unfolded Pieces 51
Finding Pieces for the Same Unfolded Pieces 52, 53
TEACHING SUGGESTIONS AND ANSWERS 54-62

FINDING A LINE OF SYMMETRY

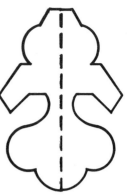

If you fold on the dotted line, the two halves of this design will match.

This dotted line is called a <u>vertical line of symmetry</u>.

Each of these designs has a <u>horizontal line of symmetry,</u> as shown by the dotted lines.

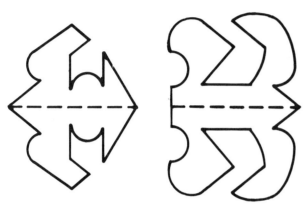

Neither of these designs has a line of symmetry.

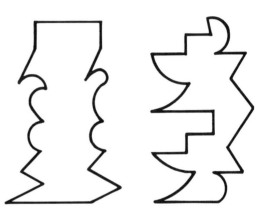

Tell what kind of symmetry each of these designs has by writing <u>vertical</u>, <u>horizontal</u>, or <u>none</u> under each figure. Use a dotted line to show the symmetry for those designs that have a line of symmetry.

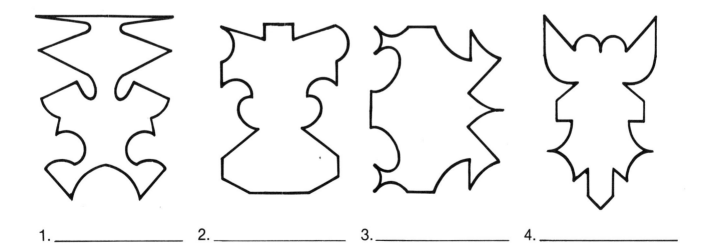

1. _____   2. _____   3. _____   4. _____

Check your answers by cutting out each figure and folding on your dotted line to see that the two halves match.

   Spatial Problem Solving with Paper Folding and Cutting © 1984 Cuisenaire Co. of America, Inc.

FINDING A LINE OF SYMMETRY

Tell what kind of symmetry each of these designs has by writing <u>vertical</u>, <u>horizontal</u>, or <u>none</u> under each figure. Use a dotted line to show the symmetry for those designs that have a line of symmetry. The first design has been done for you.

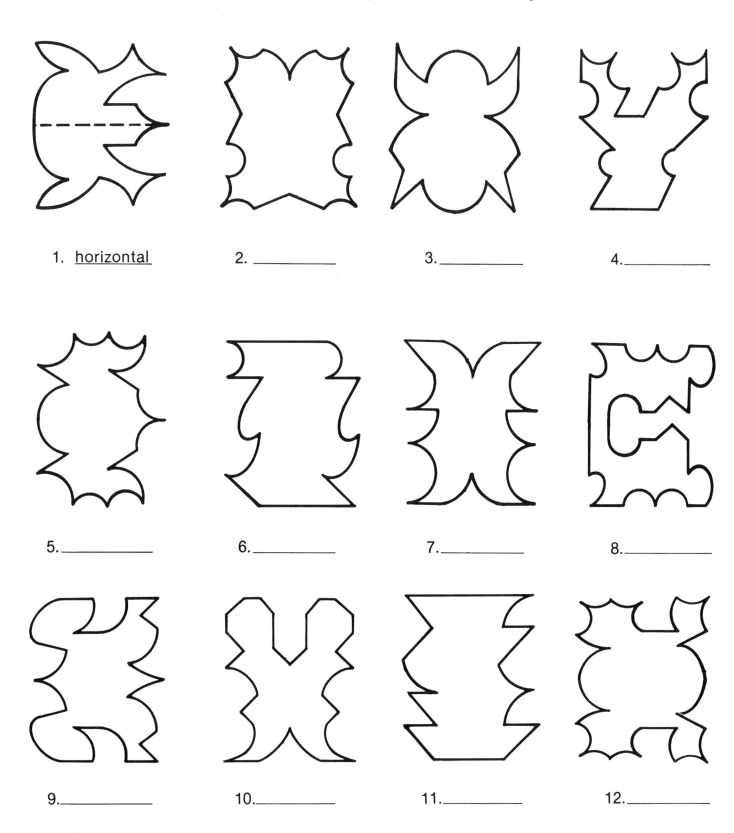

1. <u>horizontal</u>

2. _____

3. _____

4. _____

5. _____

6. _____

7. _____

8. _____

9. _____

10. _____

11. _____

12. _____

MAKING DESIGNS WITH VERTICAL FOLDS

When a design has a line of symmetry, it can be cut from a folded piece of paper. Here is how it is done.

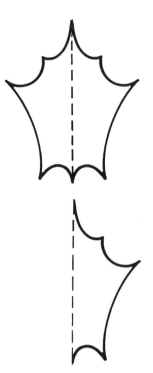

First, see if the design has a line of symmetry.

This design has a <u>vertical</u> line of symmetry, as shown by the dotted line.

Next cut out the design and fold it on the line of symmetry.

Place this folded piece on a sheet of paper that has been folded in half vertically. Make sure to place the line of symmetry (fold line) of the design along the fold line of the paper.

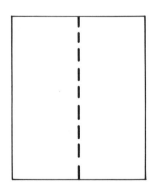

Sheet of Paper

Folded
Line

Folded Sheet of Paper

Folded Design Placed on the Folded Paper

Trace around the piece; then cut along the tracing line, keeping the paper folded.

Now unfold this piece and see that it matches the original design.

 Spatial Problem Solving with Paper Folding and Cutting © 1984 Cuisenaire Co. of America, Inc.

MAKING DESIGNS WITH HORIZONTAL FOLDS

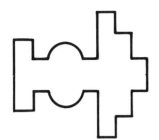

Could this design be cut from a folded piece of paper?
Let's try it.

First, find the line of symmetry.

This design has a <u>horizontal</u> line of symmetry, as shown
by the dotted line.

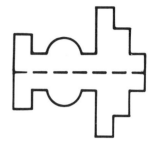

Next cut out the design and fold it on the line
of symmetry.

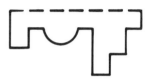

Place this folded piece on a sheet of paper that has been folded in half horizontally.
Make sure to place the line of symmetry (fold line) of the design along the fold line
of the paper.

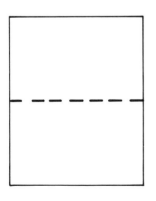

Sheet of Paper

Fold Line

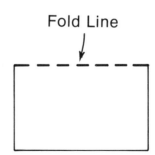

Folded Sheet of Paper

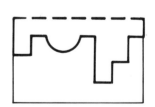

Folded Design Placed
on Folded Paper

Trace around the piece; then cut along the tracing line,
keeping the paper folded.

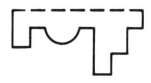

Now unfold this piece and see that it matches the
original design.

MATCHING A GIVEN DESIGN AND ITS FOLDED PIECE

Each design in the left hand column can be cut from a folded piece of paper.
Which of the five drawings on the right is the correct folded piece for the design
on the left? Circle the letter for the correct piece.
Caution: Note that the folded piece has to be placed correctly on the folded paper!

Spatial Problem Solving with Paper Folding and Cutting © 1984 Cuisenaire Co. of America, Inc.

MATCHING A GIVEN DESIGN AND ITS FOLDED PIECE

Each design in the left hand column can be cut from a folded piece of paper.
Which of the five drawings on the right is the correct folded piece for the design
on the left? Circle the letter for the correct piece.
Caution: Note that the folded piece has to be placed correctly on the folded paper!

MATCHING DESIGNS AND FOLDED PIECES

Each design at the top of the page can be cut from a folded piece of paper. Which of the drawings at the bottom of the page is the correct folded piece for each design at the top? Write the correct letter next to each numeral.

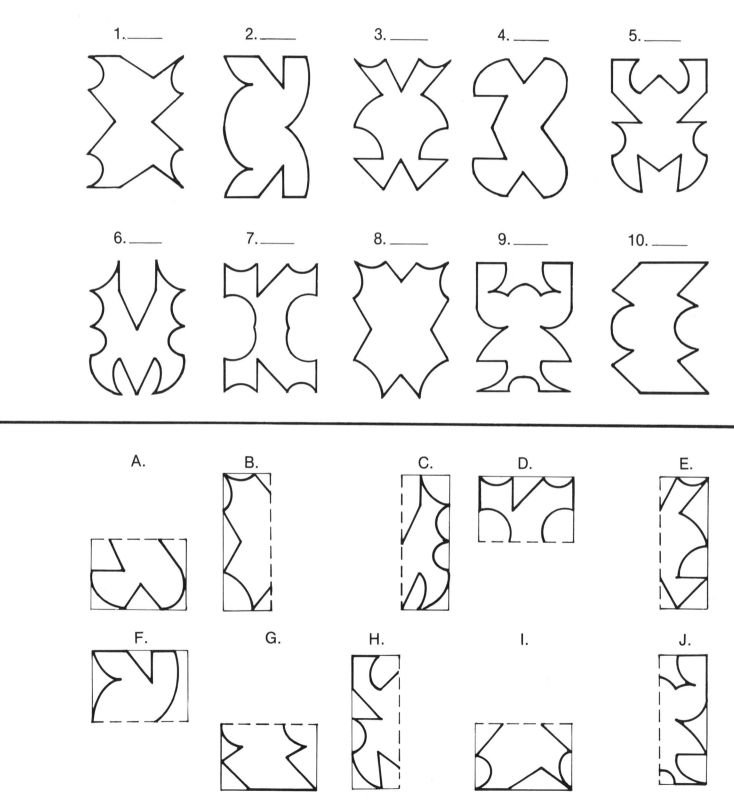

Spatial Problem Solving with Paper Folding and Cutting © 1984 Cuisenaire Co. of America, Inc.

MATCHING DESIGNS AND FOLDED PIECES

Each design at the top of the page can be cut from a folded piece of paper. Which of the drawings at the bottom of the page is the correct folded piece for each design at the top? Write the correct letter next to each numeral.

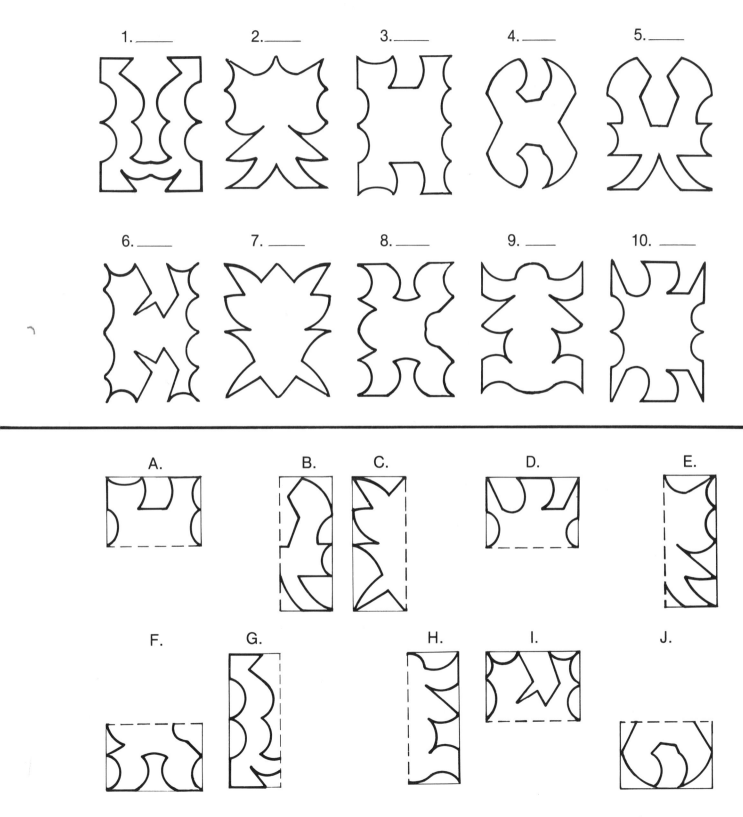

FINDING POSSIBLE FOLDED PIECES FOR A GIVEN DESIGN

Each of the designs in the left hand column can be cut by using <u>none</u>, <u>one</u>, or <u>more</u> of the folded pieces in the right hand column. Find all the possible answers and circle the letters for the correct pieces. Write <u>none</u> in the right hand column if no piece is correct.

Caution: Note that the folded piece has to be placed correctly on the folded paper!

SPATIAL PROBLEM SOLVING with Paper Folding and Cutting © 1984 Cuisenaire Co. of America, Inc.

FINDING POSSIBLE FOLDED PIECES FOR A GIVEN DESIGN

Each of the designs in the left hand column can be cut by using <u>none</u>, <u>one</u>, or
<u>more</u> of the folded pieces in the right hand column. Find all the possible answers
and circle the letters for the correct pieces. Write <u>none</u> in the right hand column
if no piece is correct.
Caution: Note that the folded piece has to be placed correctly on the folded paper!

UNFOLDING A CUT-OUT PIECE

In the left hand column are pieces that have been cut from a folded sheet of paper with the fold line indicated. Which of the five drawings on the right shows the design that will result from unfolding the cut-out piece? Circle the letter above the correct design.

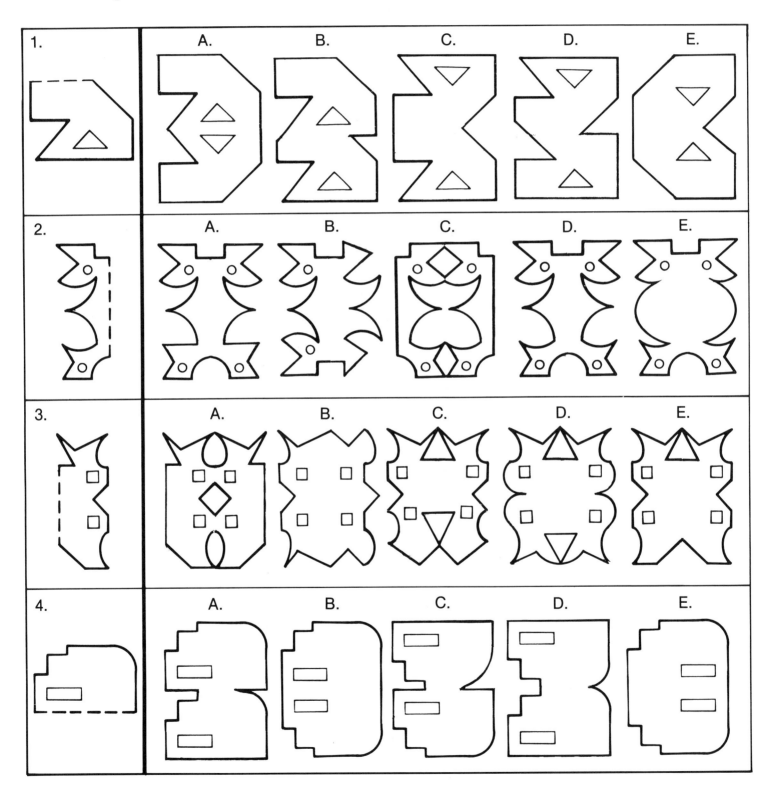

SPATIAL PROBLEM SOLVING with Paper Folding and Cutting © 1984 Cuisenaire Co. of America, Inc.

UNFOLDING A CUT-OUT PIECE

In the left hand column are pieces that have been cut from a folded sheet of paper with the fold line indicated. Which of the five drawings on the right shows the design that will result from unfolding the cut-out piece? Circle the letter above the correct design.

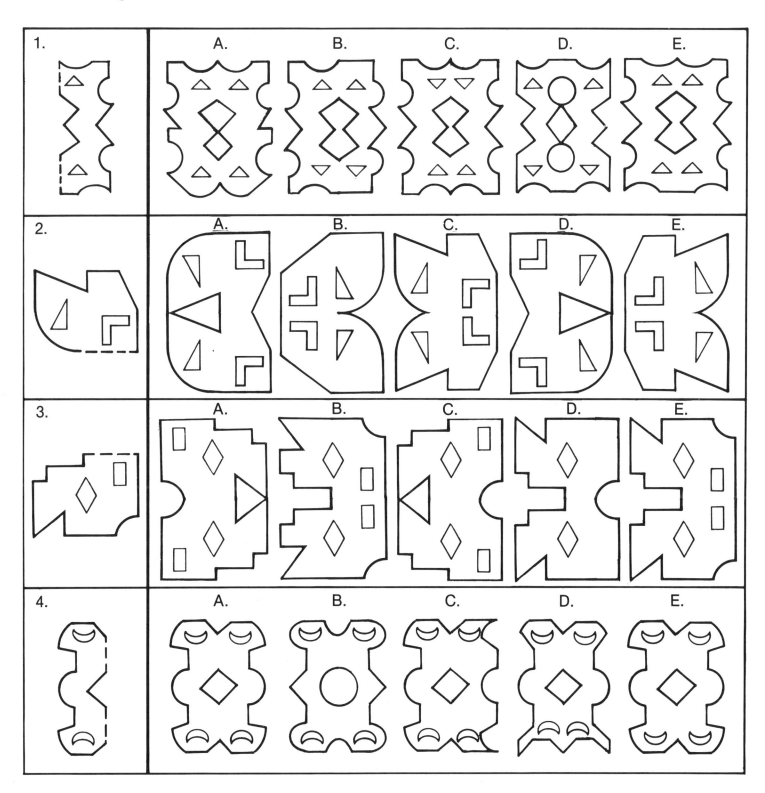

MATCHING CUT-OUTS AND UNFOLDED PIECES

At the top of the page are pieces that have been cut from a sheet of paper with the fold lines indicated. Which of the drawings at the bottom of the page shows the design that will result from unfolding each piece? Write the correct letter next to each numeral.

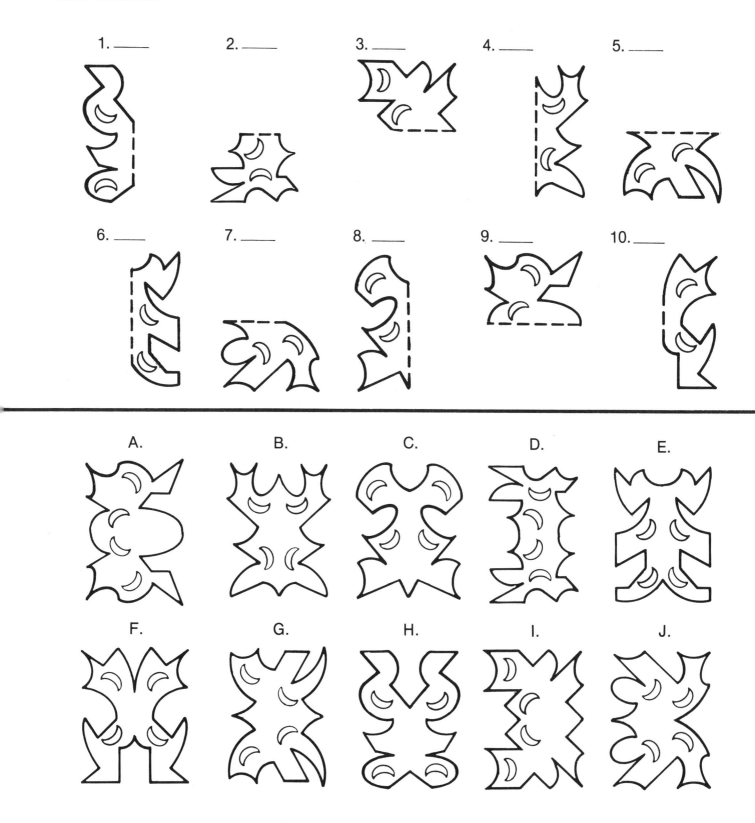

Spatial Problem Solving with Paper Folding and Cutting © 1984 Cuisenaire Co. of America, Inc.

MATCHING CUT-OUTS AND UNFOLDED PIECES

At the top of the page are pieces that have been cut from a sheet of paper with the fold lines indicated. Which of the drawings at the bottom of the page shows the design that will result from unfolding each piece? Write the correct letter next to each numeral.

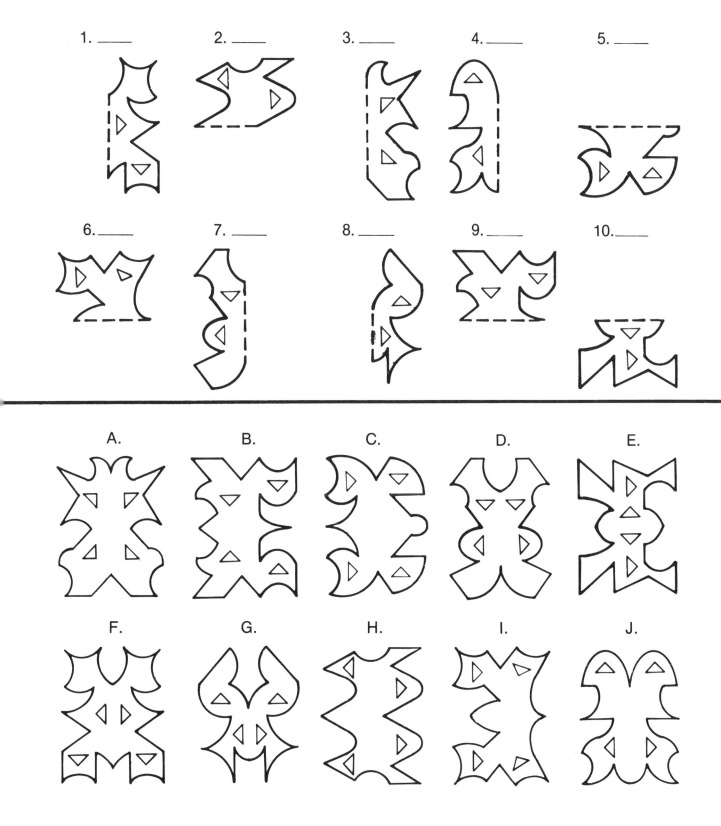

FINDING THE UNFOLDED PIECE

Look at each piece in the left hand column to see if it would unfold on the dotted line into any of the designs in the right hand column. It may be the case that none of the designs in the right hand column is correct. Either write none in the right hand column, or circle the letter above the correct design.

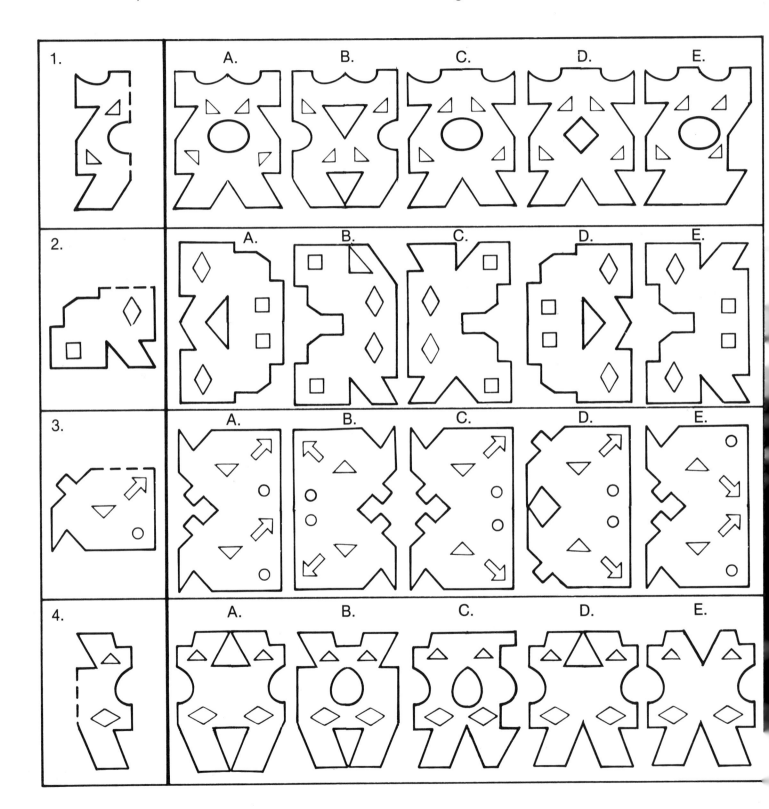

Spatial Problem Solving with Paper Folding and Cutting © 1984 Cuisenaire Co. of America, Inc.

FINDING THE UNFOLDED PIECE

Look at each piece in the left hand column to see if it would unfold on the dotted line into any of the designs in the right hand column. It may be the case that none of the designs in the right hand column is correct. Either write none in the right hand column, or circle the letter above the correct design.

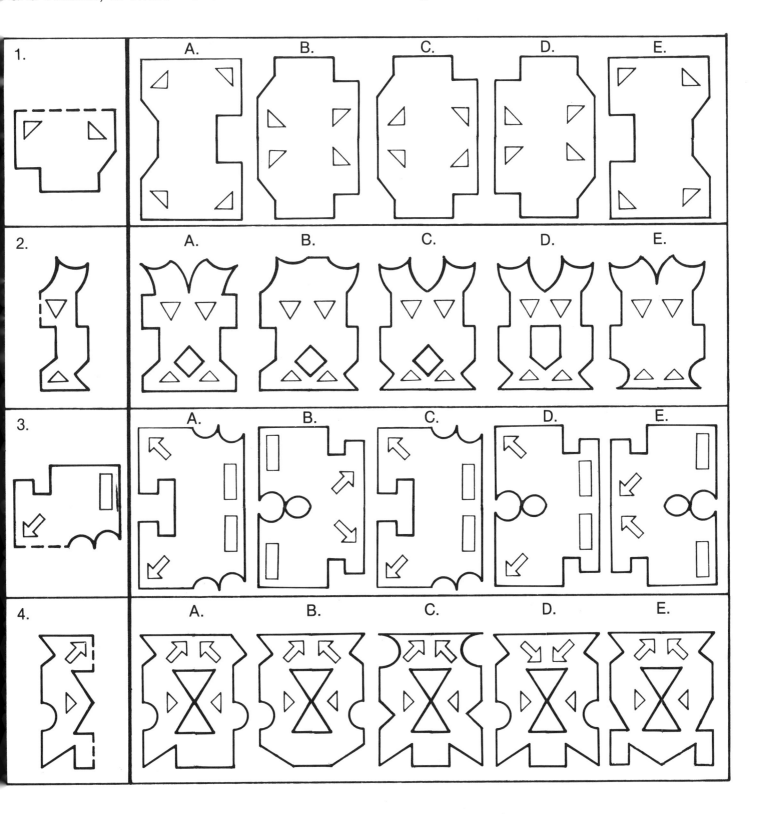

DRAWING UNFOLDED DESIGNS

Draw the design that you would get if you unfolded each of the given pieces on the dotted line.

1.

2.

3.

4.

5.

6.

DRAWING UNFOLDED DESIGNS

Draw the design that you would get if you unfolded each of the given pieces on the dotted line.

1.

2.

3.

4.

5.

6.

MATCHING PAIRS FOR THE SAME UNFOLDED DESIGN

Match pairs of pieces that would give the same design if you unfolded each on the dotted line. Write the letters of the pairs of pieces in the space provided.
Note: Some of the unfolded designs have both a horizontal and vertical line of symmetry.

A.

B.

C.

D.

E.

F.

G.

H.

I.
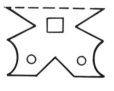

J.

K.

L.

M.

N.

O.

P.

Answers: _____ and _____   _____ and _____   _____ and _____   _____ and _____

_____ and _____   _____ and _____   _____ and _____   _____ and _____

Spatial Problem Solving with Paper Folding and Cutting © 1984 Cuisenaire Co. of America, Inc.

MATCHING PAIRS FOR THE SAME UNFOLDED DESIGN

Match pairs of pieces that would give the same design if you unfolded each on the dotted line. Write the letters of the pairs of pieces in the space provided.
Note: Some of the unfolded designs have both a horizontal and vertical line of symmetry.

A.

B.

C.

D.

E.

F.

G.

H.

I.

J.

K.

L.

M.

N.

O.

P.

Answers: _____ and _____   _____ and _____   _____ and _____   _____ and _____

_____ and _____   _____ and _____   _____ and _____   _____ and _____

FINDING TWO LINES OF SYMMETRY

If you fold on both dotted lines, the four quarters of the design will match. The original design has two lines of symmetry.

The design has both a <u>vertical</u> and <u>horizontal</u> line of symmetry.

Tell how many lines of symmetry each of these designs has by writing 0, 1, or 2 under each figure. Use dotted lines to show the symmetry.

1. _____   2. _____   3. _____   4. _____

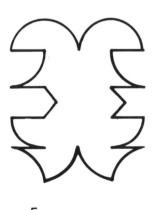

5. _____   6. _____   7. _____   8. _____

Try this: Check your answers by cutting out the figures and folding on the dotted lines. Experiment to see that when there are two lines of symmetry, it does not matter which one you fold first.

   Spatial Problem Solving with Paper Folding and Cutting © 1984 Cuisenaire Co. of America, Inc.

FINDING LINES OF SYMMETRY

Tell how many lines of symmetry each of these designs has by writing 0, 1, or 2 under each figure. Use dotted lines to show the symmetry.

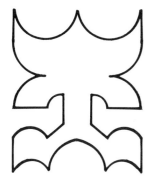

1. _____

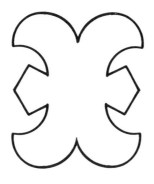

2. _____

3. _____

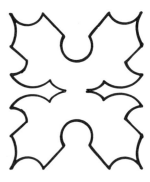

4. _____

5. _____

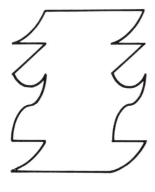

6. _____

7. _____

8. _____

9. _____

10. _____

11. _____

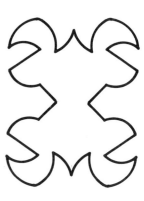

12. _____

MAKING DESIGNS USING TWO LINES OF SYMMETRY

When a design has both a horizontal and vertical line of symmetry, it can be cut from a piece of paper that has been folded twice.

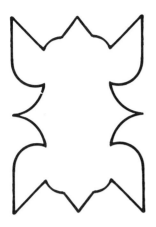

This can be done in any one of the following four ways:

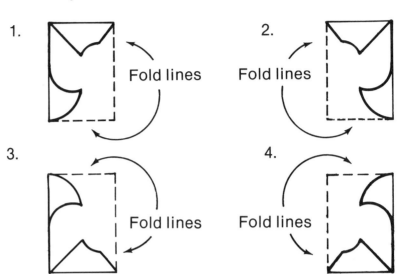

1.
Fold lines

2.
Fold lines

3.
Fold lines

4.
Fold lines

Which of the five drawings on the right is the correct folded piece for the design on the left? Circle the letter above the correct piece.

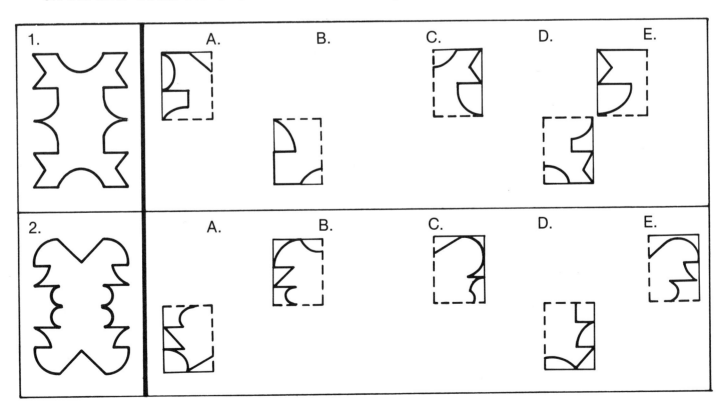

1.

A.   B.   C.   D.   E.

2.

A.   B.   C.   D.   E.

Spatial Problem Solving with Paper Folding and Cutting © 1984 Cuisenaire Co. of America, Inc.

MATCHING A GIVEN DESIGN AND ITS DOUBLY FOLDED PIECE

Each design in the left hand column can be cut from a doubly folded piece of paper. Which of the five drawings is the correct folded piece for the design on the left? Circle the letter above for correct piece. Caution: Note that the two lines of symmetry have to be placed along the folds of the paper.

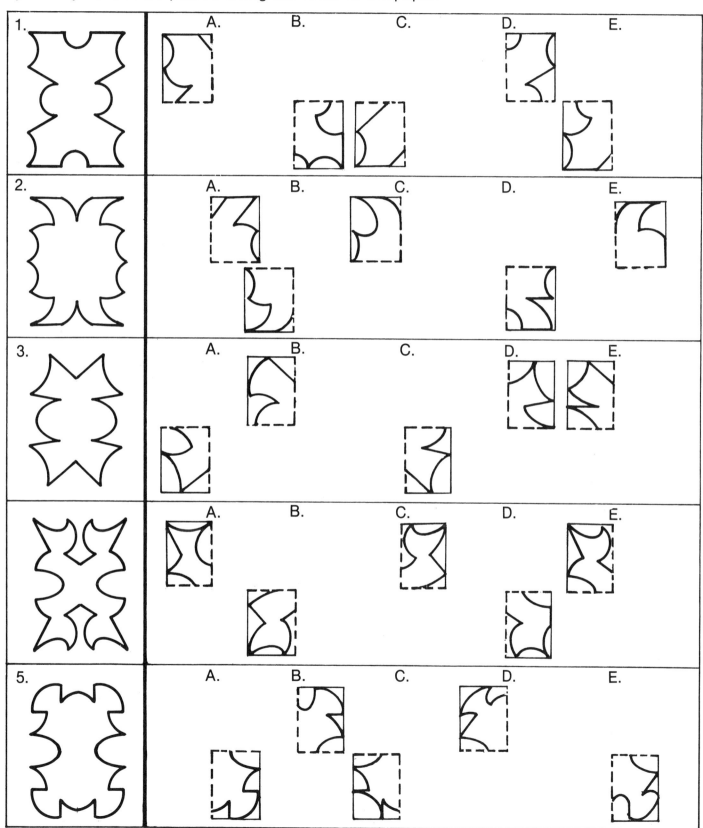

MATCHING A GIVEN DESIGN AND ITS DOUBLY FOLDED PIECE

Each design in the left hand column can be cut from a doubly folded piece of paper. Which of the five drawings is the correct folded piece for the design on the left? Circle the letter for the correct piece. Caution: Note that the two lines of symmetry have to be placed along the folds of the paper.

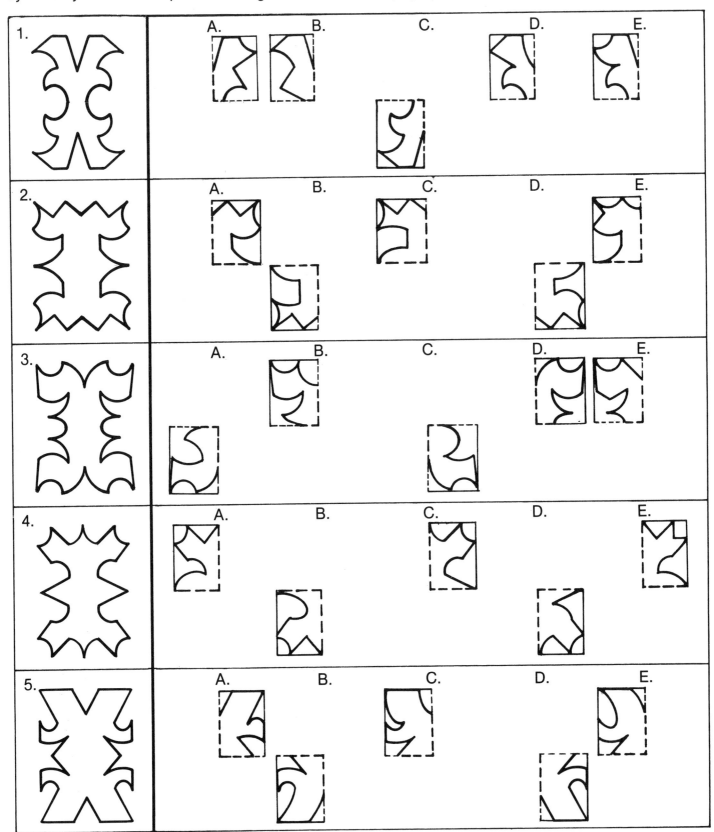

Spatial Problem Solving with Paper Folding and Cutting © 1984 Cuisenaire Co. of America, inc.

FINDING POSSIBLE FOLDED PIECES FOR A GIVEN DESIGN

Each of the designs in the left hand column can be cut by using 0, 1, 2, 3, or 4 of the folded pieces in the right hand column. Find all the possible answers and either write <u>none</u> in the right hand column, or circle the letters above the correct pieces. Caution: Note that the folded piece has to be placed correctly on the folded paper.

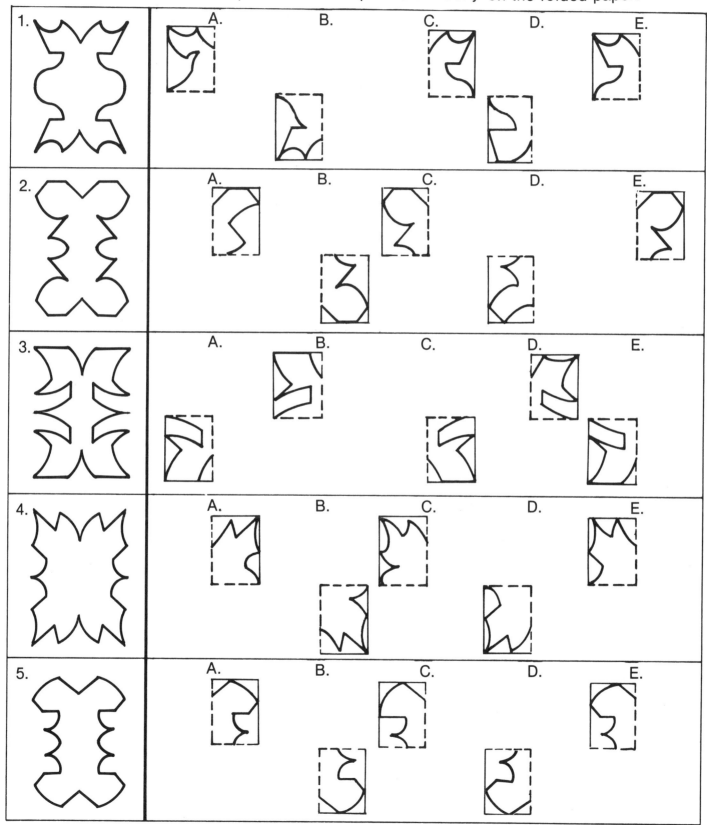

MATCHING DESIGNS AND DOUBLY FOLDED PIECES

Each design at the top of the page can be cut from a doubly folded piece of paper. Which of the drawings at the bottom of the page is the correct folded piece for each design at the top? Write the correct letter next to each numeral.

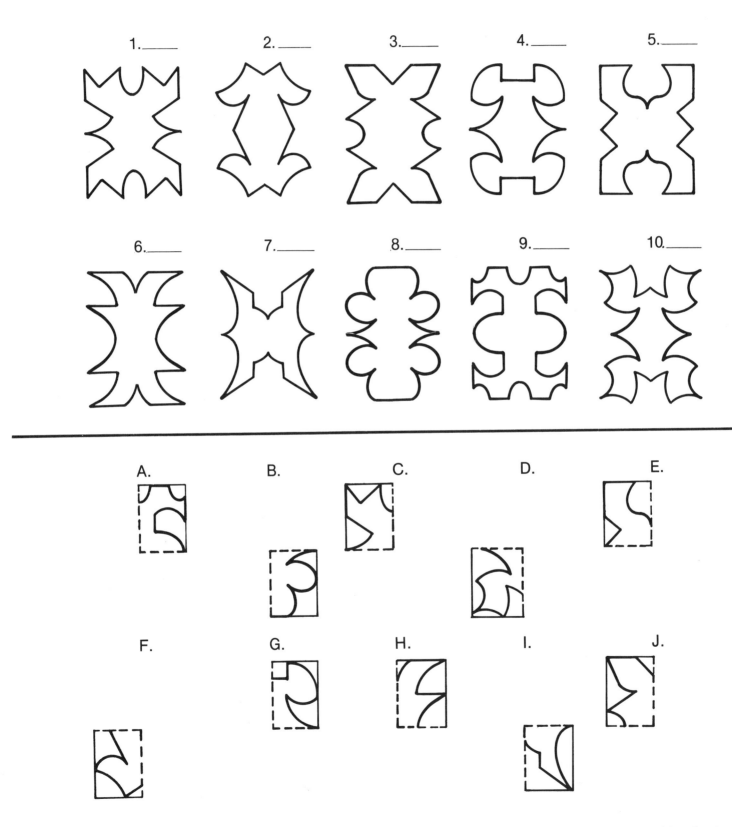

Spatial Problem Solving with Paper Folding and Cutting © 1984 Cuisenaire Co. of America, Inc.

MATCHING DESIGNS AND DOUBLY FOLDED PIECES

Each design at the top of the page can be cut from a doubly folded piece of paper.
Which of the drawings at the bottom of the page is the correct folded piece for
each design at the top? Write the correct letter next to each numeral.

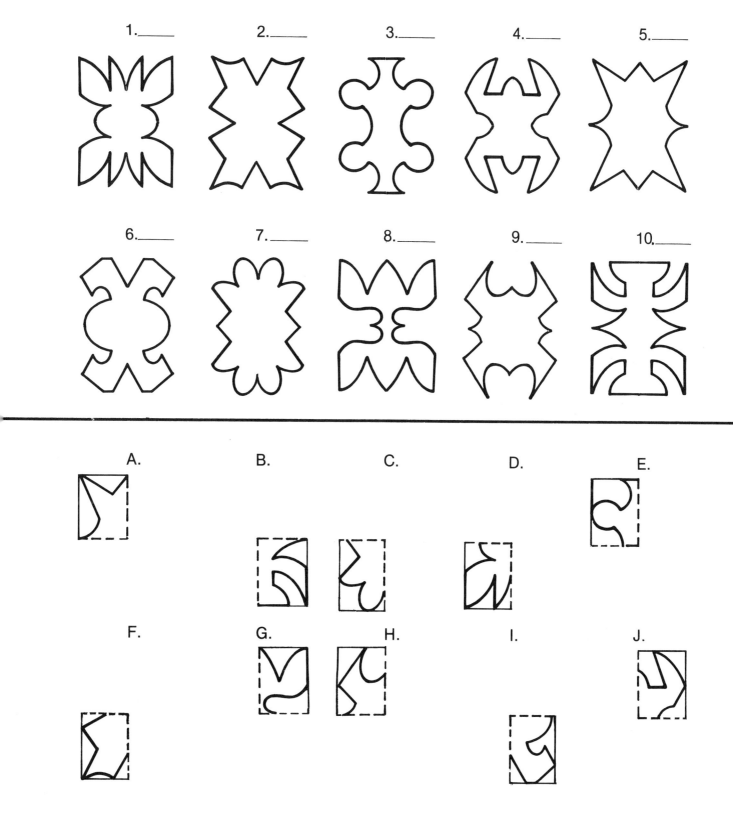

1.____ 2.____ 3.____ 4.____ 5.____

6.____ 7.____ 8.____ 9.____ 10.____

A. B. C. D. E.

F. G. H. I. J.

FINDING POSSIBLE FOLDED PIECES FOR A GIVEN DESIGN

Each of the designs in the left hand column can be cut by using 0, 1, 2, 3, or 4 of the folded pieces in the right hand column. Find all the possible answers and either write <u>none</u> in the right hand column, or circle the letters above the correct piece. Caution: Note that the folded piece has to be placed on the folded paper.

		A.	B.	C.	D.	E.
1.						
2.						
3.						
4.						
5.						

Spatial Problem Solving with Paper Folding and Cutting © 1984 Cuisenaire Co. of America, Inc.

FINDING POSSIBLE FOLDED PIECES FOR A GIVEN DESIGN

Each of the designs in the left hand column can be cut by using 0, 1, 2, 3, or 4 of
the folded pieces in the right hand column. Find all the possible answers and
either write <u>none</u> in the right hand column, or circle the letters above the correct piece.
Caution: Note that the folded piece has to be placed on the folded paper.

		A.	B.	C.	D.	E.
1.						
2.						
3.						
4.						
5.						

UNFOLDING A CUT-OUT PIECE

In the left hand column are pieces that have been cut from a doubly folded sheet of paper with the fold lines dotted in. Which of the five drawings on the right shows the design that will result from unfolding the cut-out piece? Circle the correct letter above the given design.

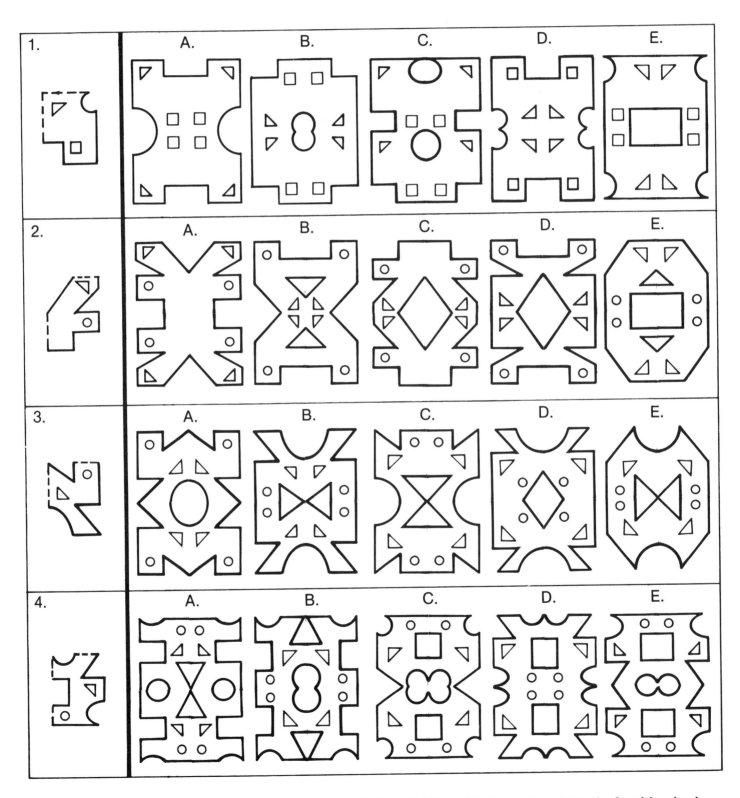

Spatial Problem Solving with Paper Folding and Cutting © 1984 Cuisenaire Co. of America, Inc.

UNFOLDING A CUT-OUT PIECE

In the left hand column are pieces that have been cut from a doubly folded sheet of paper with the fold lines dotted in. Which of the five drawings on the right shows the design that will result from unfolding the cut-out piece? Circle the correct letter above the given design.

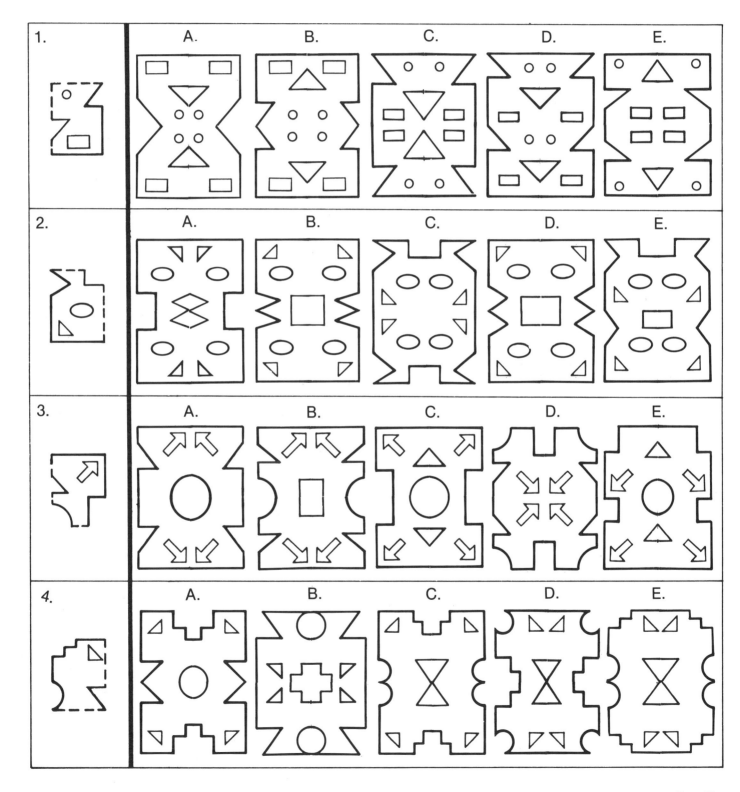

MATCHING CUT-OUTS AND UNFOLDED PIECES

At the top of the page are pieces that have been cut from a doubly folded sheet of paper with the fold lines dotted in. Which of the drawings at the bottom of the page shows the design that will result from unfolding each piece? Write the correct letter next to each numeral.

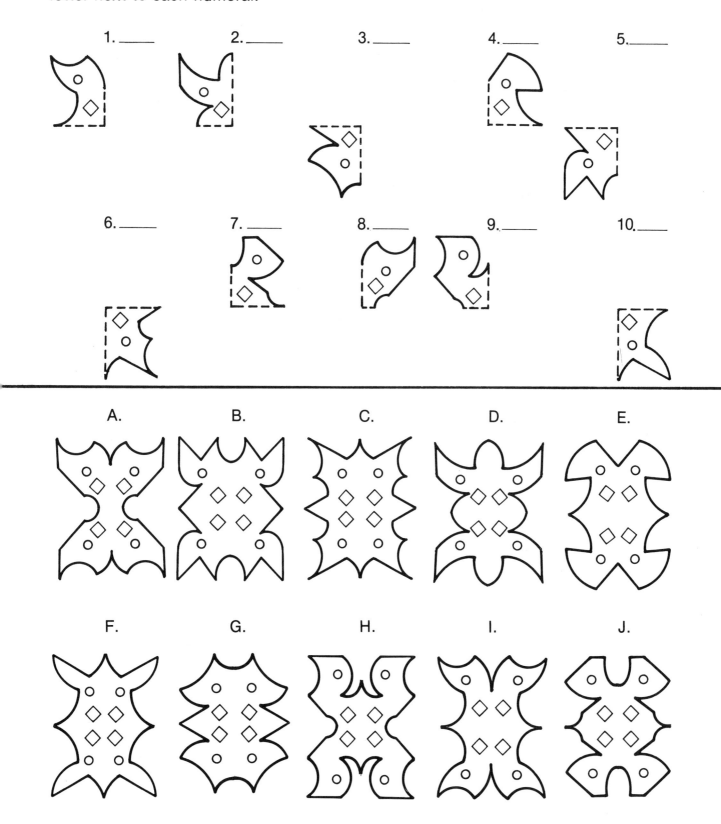

Spatial Problem Solving with Paper Folding and Cutting © 1984 Cuisenaire Co. of America, Inc.

MATCHING CUT-OUTS AND UNFOLDED PIECES

At the top of the page are pieces that have been cut from a doubly folded sheet of paper with the fold lines dotted in. Which of the drawings at the bottom of the page shows the design that will result from unfolding each piece? Write the correct letter next to each numeral.

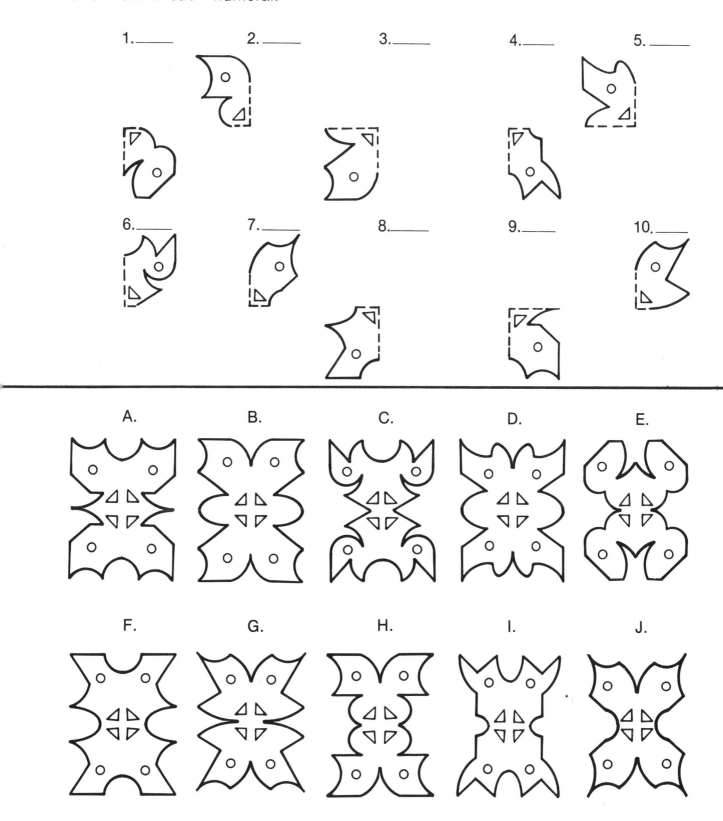

FINDING THE UNFOLDED PIECE

Look at each piece in the left hand column to see if it would unfold on the dotted lines into any of the pieces in the right hand column. It may be the case that none of the designs in the right hand column is correct. Either write <u>none</u> in the right hand column, or circle the letter above the correct design.

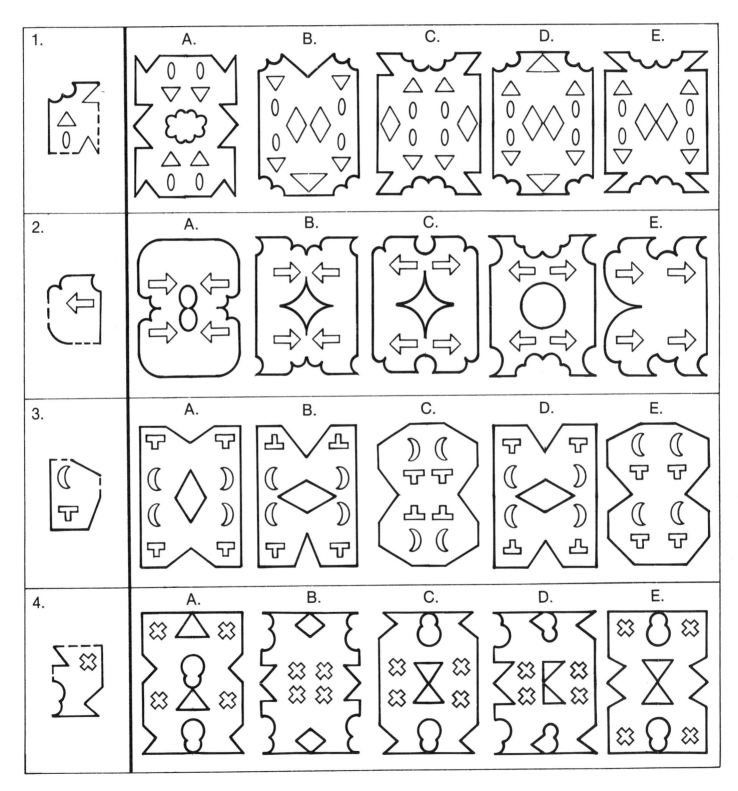

Spatial Problem Solving with Paper Folding and Cutting © 1984 Cuisenaire Co. of America, Inc.

FINDING THE UNFOLDED PIECE

Look at each piece in the left hand column to see if it would unfold on the dotted lines into any of the pieces in the right hand column. It may be the case that none of the designs in the right hand column is correct. Either write <u>none</u> in the right hand column, or circle the letter above the correct design.

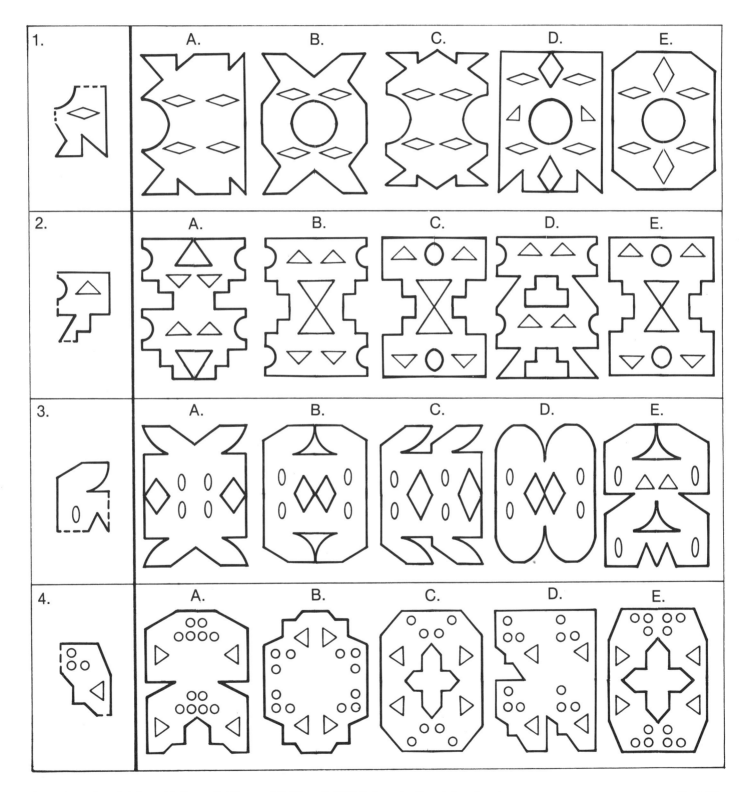

DRAWING UNFOLDED DESIGNS

Draw the design that you would get if you unfolded each of the given doubly folded pieces on the dotted lines.

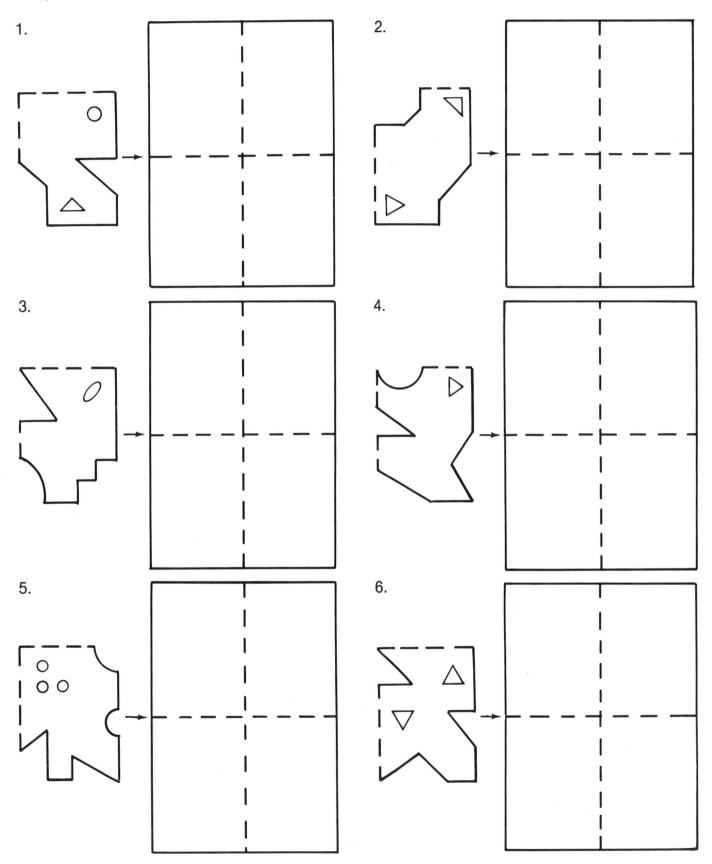

1.

2.

3.

4.

5.

6.

Spatial Problem Solving with Paper Folding and Cutting © 1984 Cuisenaire Co. of America, Inc.

DRAWING UNFOLDED DESIGNS

Draw the design that you would get if you unfolded each of the given doubly folded pieces on the dotted lines.

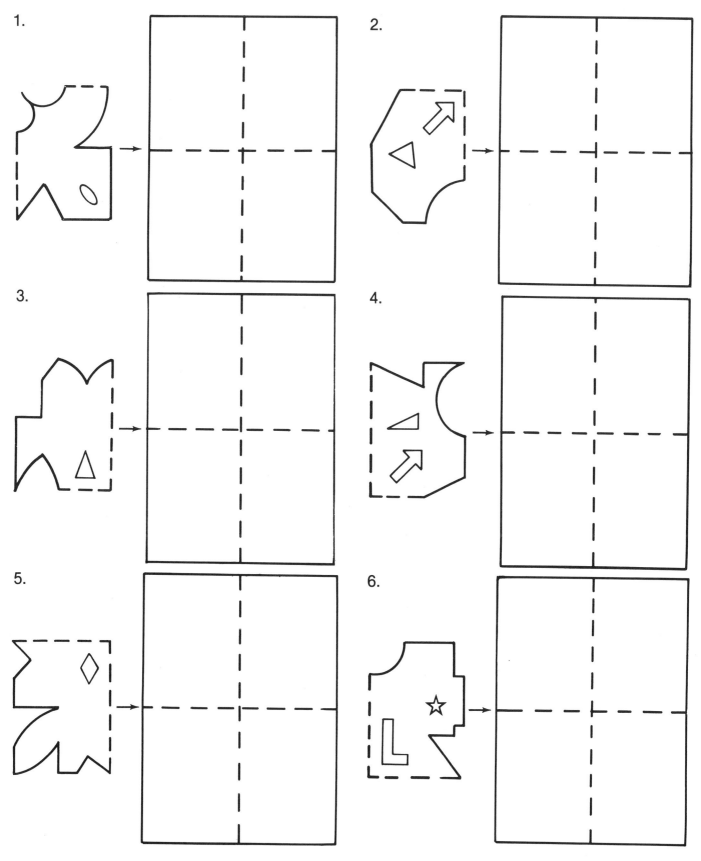

MATCHING PAIRS FOR THE SAME UNFOLDED DESIGN

Match pairs of pieces that would give the same design if you unfolded each on the dotted lines. Write the letters of the pairs of pieces in the space provided.

A.

B.

C.

D.

E.

F.

G.

H.

I.

J.

K.

L.

M.

N.

O.

P.

Answers: _____ and _____   _____ and _____   _____ and _____   _____ and _____

_____ and _____   _____ and _____   _____ and _____   _____ and _____

SPATIAL Problem Solving with Paper Folding and Cutting © 1984 Cuisenaire Co. of America, Inc.

MATCHING PAIRS FOR THE SAME UNFOLDED DESIGN

Match pairs of pieces that would give the same design if you unfolded each on the dotted lines. Write the letters of the pairs of pieces in the space provided.

A.

B.

C.

D.

E.

F.

G.

H.
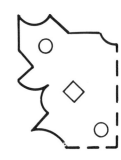

I.

J.

K.

L.

M.

N.
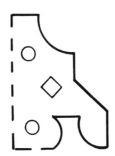

O.
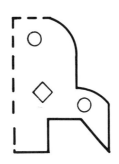

P.
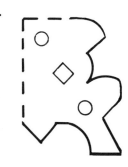

Answers: _____ and _____   _____ and _____   _____ and _____   _____ and _____

_____ and _____   _____ and _____   _____ and _____   _____ and _____

USING THREE FOLD LINES

Follow these steps to cut a design from a triply folded sheet of paper.

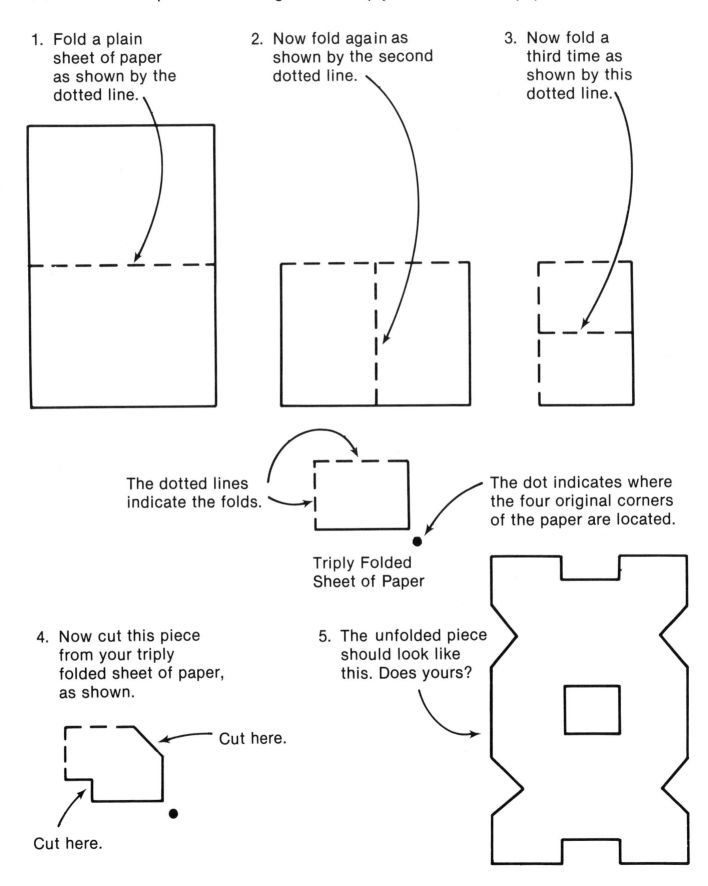

1. Fold a plain sheet of paper as shown by the dotted line.

2. Now fold again as shown by the second dotted line.

3. Now fold a third time as shown by this dotted line.

The dotted lines indicate the folds.

The dot indicates where the four original corners of the paper are located.

Triply Folded Sheet of Paper

4. Now cut this piece from your triply folded sheet of paper, as shown.

Cut here.

Cut here.

5. The unfolded piece should look like this. Does yours?

Spatial Problem Solving with Paper Folding and Cutting © 1984 Cuisenaire Co. of America, Inc.

MATCHING CUT-OUTS AND UNFOLDED PIECES

Each design at the top of the page can be cut from a triply folded piece of paper. Which of the drawings at the bottom of the page is the correct folded piece for each design at the top? Write the correct letter next to each numeral.

Remember:
The dotted lines indicate the fold lines. The dot indicates where the four original corners of the paper are located.

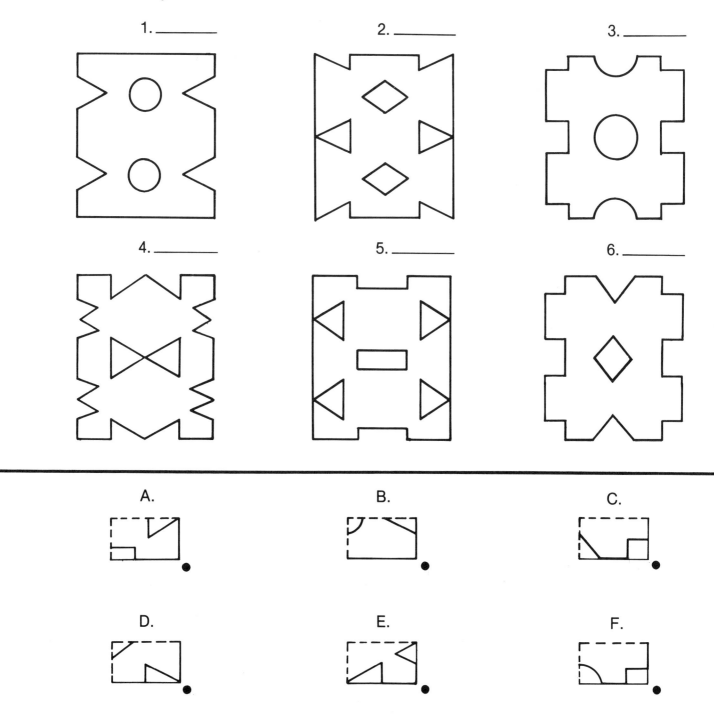

MATCHING A GIVEN DESIGN AND ITS TRIPLY FOLDED PIECE

Each design in the left hand column can be cut from a triply folded piece of paper. Which of the five drawings on the right is the correct folded piece for the design on the left? Circle the letter above the correct piece.

Remember: The dotted lines indicate the fold lines. The dot indicates where the four original corners of the paper are located.

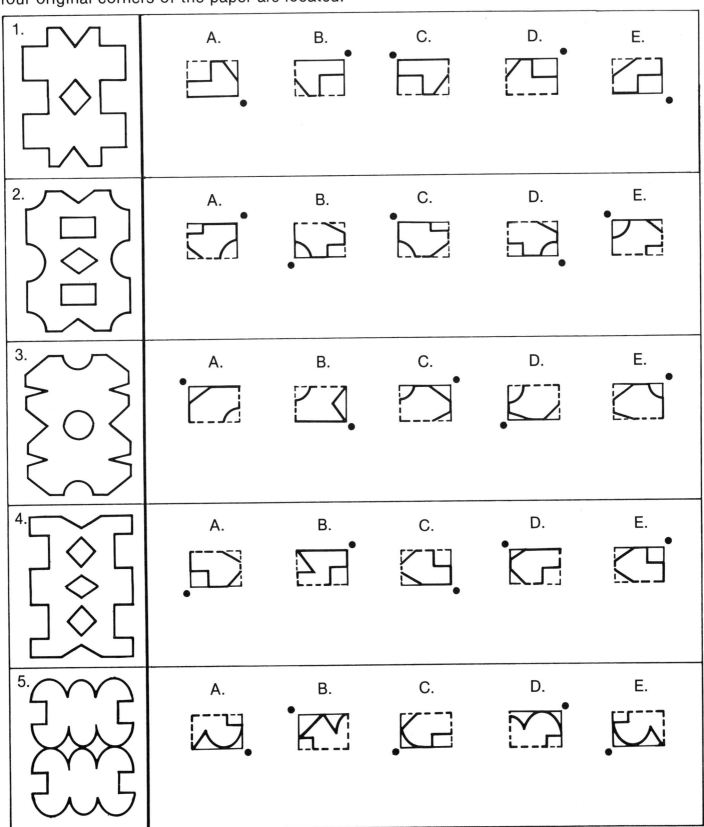

Spatial Problem Solving with Paper Folding and Cutting © 1984 Cuisenaire Co. of America, Inc.

FINDING POSSIBLE TRIPLY FOLDED PIECES FOR A GIVEN DESIGN

Each of the designs in the left hand column can be cut by using none, one, or more of the triply folded pieces in the right hand column. Find all the possible answers and either write <u>none</u> in the right hand column, or circle the letters of the correct pieces. Remember: The dotted lines indicate the fold lines. The dot indicates where the four original corners of the paper are located.

1.	A.	B.	C.	D.	E.
2.	A.	B.	C.	D.	E.
3.	A.	B.	C.	D.	E.
4.	A.	B.	C.	D.	E.
5.	A.	B.	C.	D.	E.

FINDING THE UNFOLDED PIECE

Match each triply folded piece from the left hand column with the correct unfolded design in the right hand column. Circle the letter above the correct design.

Remember: The solid dot shows the corner where the four original corners of the paper are now located.

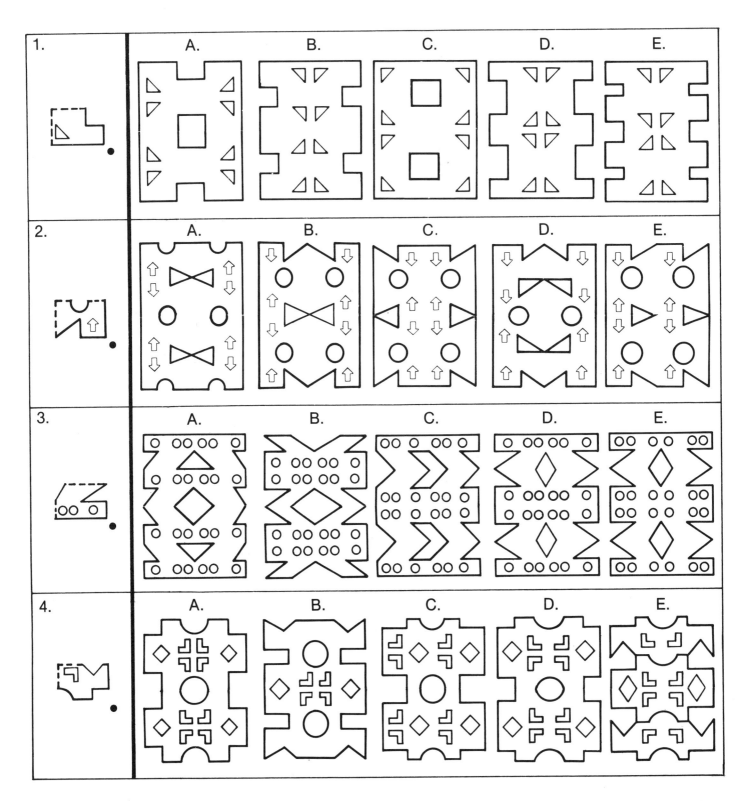

Spatial Problem Solving with Paper Folding and Cutting © 1984 Cuisenaire Co. of America, Inc.

FINDING THE UNFOLDED PIECE

Match each triply folded piece from the left hand column with the correct unfolded design in the right hand column. Circle the letter above the correct design.

Remember: The solid dot shows the corner where the four original corners of the paper are now located.

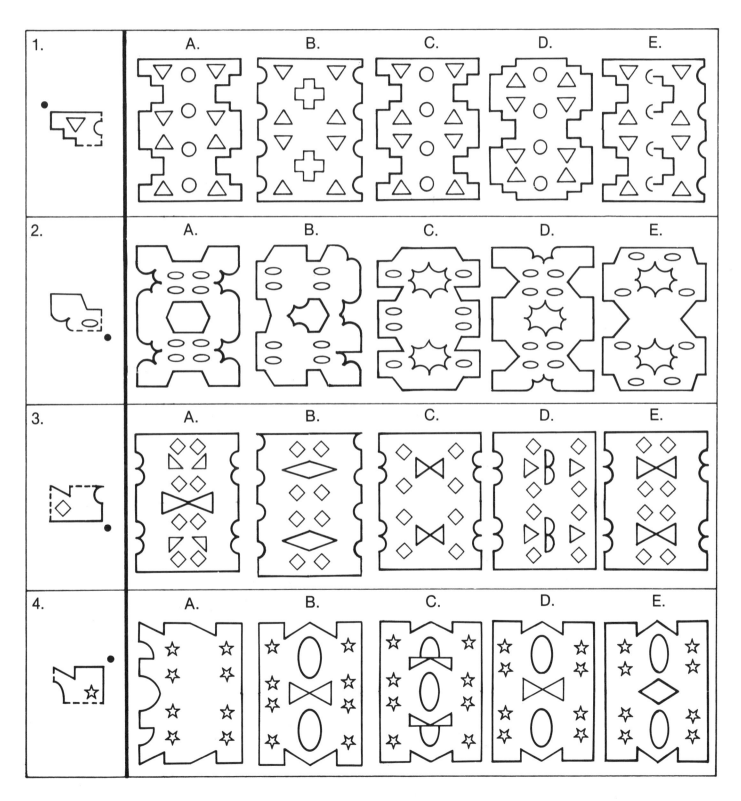

DRAWING UNFOLDED DESIGNS

Draw the design that you would get if you unfolded each of the given triply folded pieces on the dotted lines. Remember that the solid dot shows the corner where the four original corners of the paper are located.

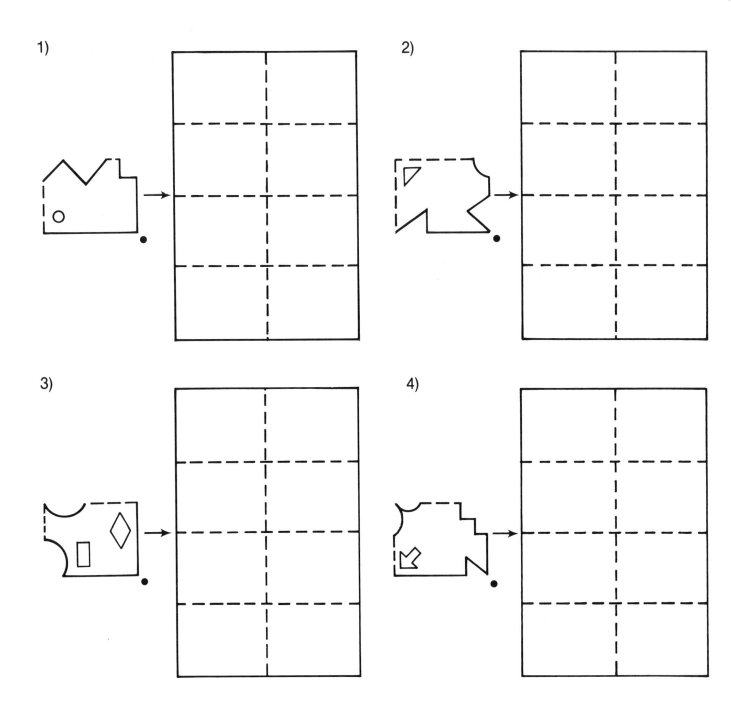

1)

2)

3)

4)

You may wish to fold a plain piece of paper three times and make the indicated cuts to help see the unfolded piece.

DRAWING UNFOLDED DESIGNS

Draw the design that you would get if you unfolded each of the given triply folded pieces on the dotted lines. Remember that the solid dot shows the corner where the four original corners of the paper are located.

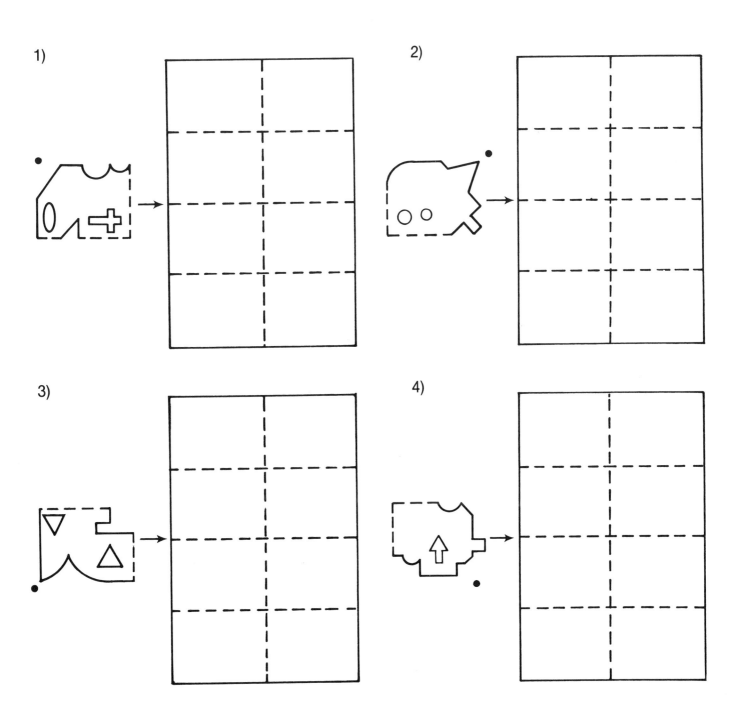

1)

2)

3)

4)

You may wish to fold a plain piece of paper three times and make the indicated cuts to help see the unfolded piece.

ROTATING AND REFLECTING PIECES

Each of the designs in the left hand column can be cut from each of the three folded pieces in the right hand column. Note that the pieces in the right hand column have been changed from their usual orientations by rotations and/or reflections. For each piece, tell how many fold lines are involved. Then describe in your own words what rotations and/or reflections you see. More than one description may be possible for each piece.

1.

A.

Description:
One horizontal
fold line.
Bottom half rotated.

B.

Description:

C.

Description:

2.

A.

Description:

B.

Description:

C.

Description:

3.

A.

Description:

B.

Description:

C.

Description:

Spatial Problem Solving with Paper Folding and Cutting © 1984 Cuisenaire Co. of America, Inc.

MATCHING DESIGNS WITH ROTATED AND REFLECTED PIECES

Each of the designs at the top of the page can be cut from one or more of the rotated and/or reflected pieces at the bottom of the page. Write the correct letters next to each numeral. Not all of the pieces at the bottom of the page can be used.

1. _____ 2. _____ 3. _____ 4. _____ 5. _____

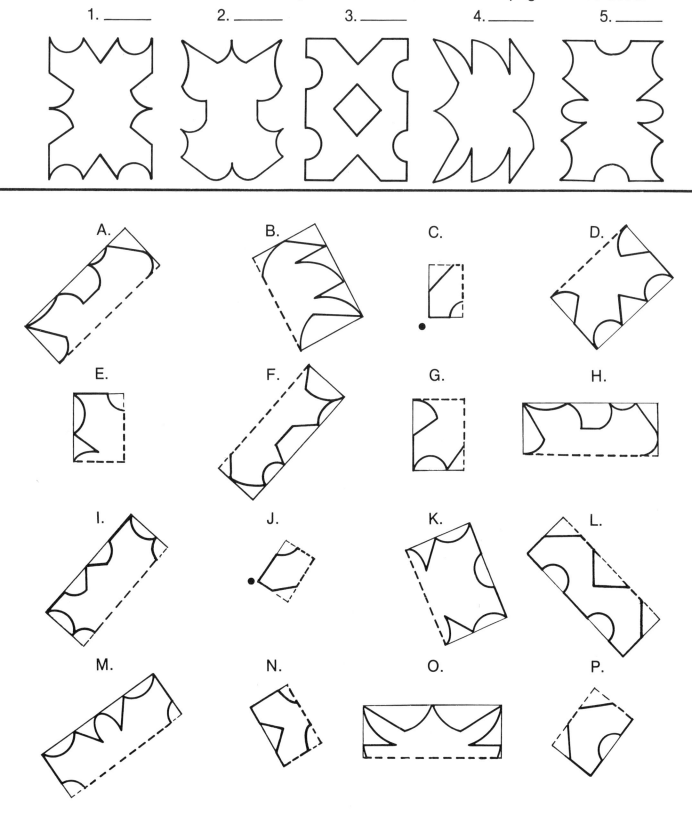

MATCHING CUT-OUTS AND UNFOLDED PIECES

At the top of the page are pieces that have been cut from folded paper and then rotated and/or reflected to change the orientation. Which of the designs at the bottom of the page shows the design that will result from reorienting and unfolding each piece according to the fold lines indicated? Write the correct letter or the word none next to each numeral.

Note: Not all of the pieces at the top have answers at the bottom.

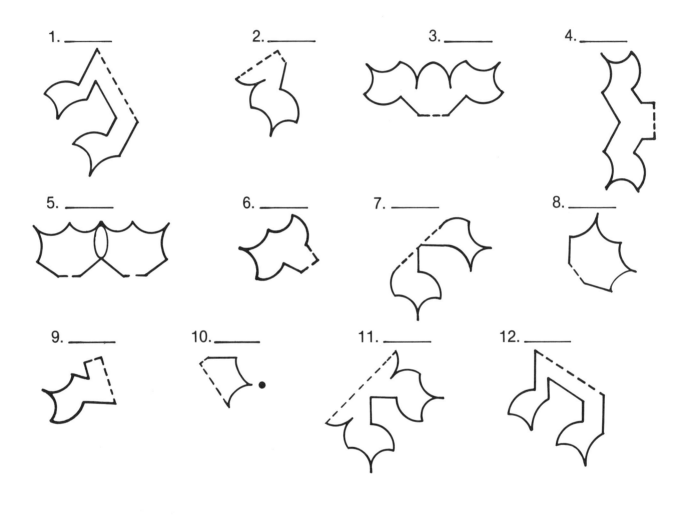

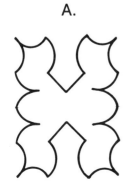

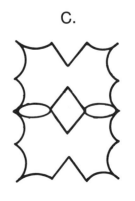

Spatial Problem Solving with Paper Folding and Cutting © 1984 Cuisenaire Co. of America, Inc.

FINDING PIECES FOR THE SAME UNFOLDED PIECES

Sort the pieces below to find the ones that will give the same design if you rotated and/or reflected the piece and then unfolded it according to the dotted lines. Write the letters of the sets of pieces that go together in the blanks provided at the bottom of the page. These are challenging!

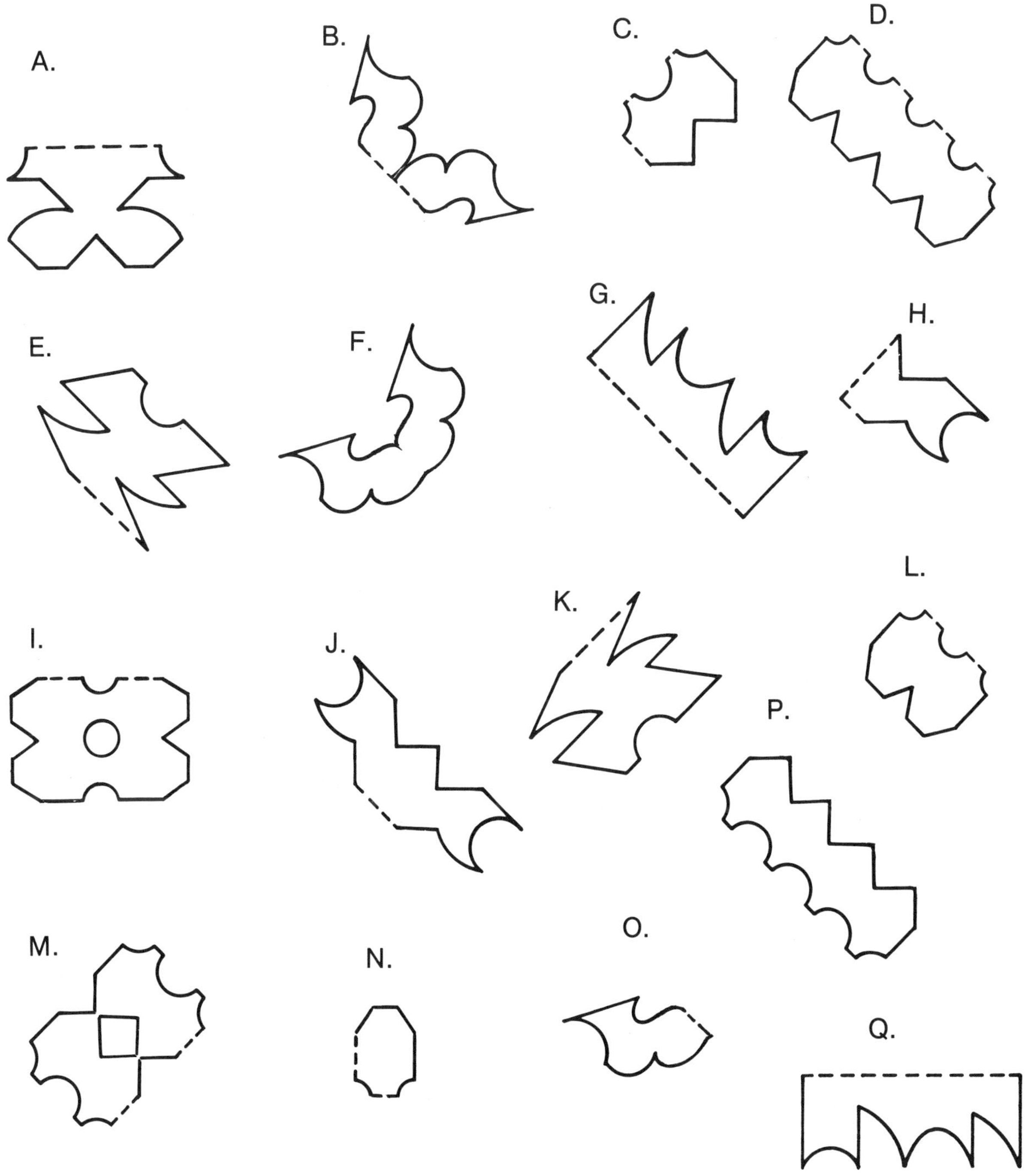

A.

B.

C.

D.

E.

F.

G.

H.

I.

J.

K.

L.

P.

M.

N.

O.

Q.

Answers:

_____   _____   _____

_____   _____   _____

FINDING PIECES FOR THE SAME UNFOLDED PIECES

Sort the pieces below to find the ones that will give the same design if you rotated and/or reflected the piece and then unfolded it according to the dotted lines. Write the letters of the sets of pieces that go together in the blanks provided at the bottom of the page. These are challenging!

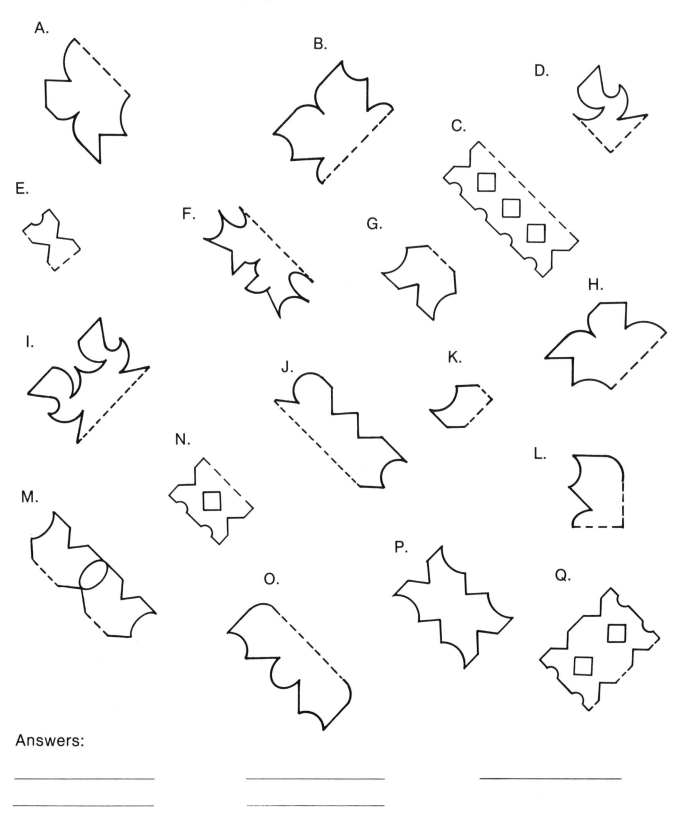

Answers:

_____   _____   _____

_____   _____

Spatial Problem Solving with Paper Folding and Cutting © 1984 Cuisenaire Co. of America, Inc.

TEACHING SUGGESTIONS AND ANSWERS

Pages 1-10: General Comments

The first ten pages of this book are devoted to whole-to-parts problems. Students are presented with a "whole" design and then are asked to find the folded "part" which could be used to cut the design from a folded piece of paper. The first four pages prepare the students for this by teaching about vertical and horizontal lines of symmetry. Some students would benefit from actually cutting their own designs from folded paper as an introductory exercise. Also if mirrors are available, students should investigate symmetry using the reflection in a mirror to provide the other "half".

The exercises on Pages 5-10 are carefully sequenced, with Pages 5-8 having unique answers, and Pages 9-10 having the possibility of no answer or multiple answers. Extensive comments are given for each of the pages to help provide a rich spatial experience for students. Students should be encouraged to share their preferred methods of approaching the problems; and these methods do vary from student-to-student! They should also be asked to discuss why the incorrect choices are wrong. The types of variations in the drawings are a valuable source for helping students to develop spatial awareness and acuity and to verbalize what they visualize.

Be prepared to find that the students who excel on these tasks may not be the same students who excel on computational tasks, and that some of your numerical whizzes may be less than good spatial problem solvers. These activities offer an important balance in the curriculum.

Page 1:

1. vertical   2. none   3. horizontal   4. vertical

Many students may already know about finding a line of symmetry. Here only vertical or horizontal lines of symmetry are introduced (no diagonal lines of symmetry). When figures are folded along a line of symmetry, the two "halves" match.

When there is a vertical line of symmetry, students may think of the "left half" being folded to match the "right half", or vice versa. With horizontal symmetry, the "bottom half" could be folded onto the "top half", or vice versa.

Students are asked to dot in the line of symmetry if the figure has one. This is important for later work when only "half" of a figure will be shown with a dotted line representing the line of symmetry.

Page 2:

1. horizontal   2. vertical   3. vertical   4. none
5. horizontal   6. none   7. vertical   8. none
9. horizontal   10. vertical   11. none   12. horizontal

Even though some students will be able to tell the kind of symmetry immediately, it is important that they draw in the dotted line to gain familiarity with the notation that will be used throughout the book for a line of symmetry.

Some students may wish to cut and fold the designs to verify the lines of symmetry. Others may wish to use a mirror. If so, they should be encouraged to see that for vertical symmetry the "left half" can be reflected onto the "right half", or vice versa; and for horizontal symmetry, the "bottom half" can be reflected onto the "top half", or vice versa. These problems are self-checking, and students should be encouraged to know how to check their own answers.

#6 is an example of a figure where something mathematically consistent has been done. It should be noted that a "slide" has been done, not a reflection.

#8 is an example where students might miss the one item of detail and be misled into thinking that there is a horizontal line of symmetry. Again, "slides" are misleading for some students.

Page 3:

This is a teaching page. The teacher may wish to use the material on this page as a demonstration model (rather than duplicating the page for the students). Students may then wish to cut their own designs from a sheet of paper folded vertically.

Note that some students will fold the paper towards them, and others will fold it away from them. It doesn't matter if they end up with the "left half" or the "right half". (Because of lack of space, only one diagram is shown.)

It is important that students understand that the dotted line in the diagram indicates the fold line.

Page 4:

This page is similar to page 3, but this time shows how to fold and cut a design with a horizontal line of symmetry.

Again, there are two ways of folding, but because of lack of space, only one diagram is shown here. Either the bottom half of the paper could be folded up or the top half of the paper could be folded down. In future pages, students have to be familiar with seeing either the "top half" or the "bottom half". Stress the importance of the dotted line indicating the fold line.

Page 5:

1. E   2. D   3. B   4. E   5. A

Students are asked to find the choice in the right hand column that is the correct folded piece for the design in the left hand column. Some students will dot in the line of symmetry for the figure in the left hand column and then will look for the correct "half". Other students may think of visually completing the pieces, perhaps even using a mirror to do so.

It is very constructive, after the correct answers have been found, to discuss why the other choices for answers are incorrect. This type of discussion will help students' visual acuity. Discussing these subtleties gives depth to the problem solving experiences.

Examples of interesting things to notice about the wrong responses:

1. A. opposite curvatures in several places.
   B. an exact copy of the bottom portion of the original design; but there is a vertical line of symmetry for the original design, not a horizontal line of symmetry.
   C. an exchange of curved and straight lines.
   D. an exact copy of the top "half" of the original design; but there is a vertical line of symmetry, not a horizontal line of symmetry for the original design.
2. A. external detail on right side.
   B. opposite curvature.
   C. an exact copy of the left portion, but there is a horizontal (not vertical) line of symmetry for the original design.
   E. an exact copy of the right portion, but there is a horizontal (not vertical) line of symmetry for the original design.
3. A. left portion, but a horizontal line of symmetry.
   C. right portion, but a horizontal line of symmetry.
   D,E. opposite curvatures.
4. A. opposite curvature.
   B. bottom portion, but vertical line of symmetry.
   C. top portion, but vertical line of symmetry.
   D. wrong location of fold line.
5. B. right portion, but horizontal line of symmetry.
   C. wrong location of fold line.
   D. left portion, but horizontal line of symmetry.
   E. opposite curvatures.

Page 6:

1. D   2. E   3. C   4. D   5. B

This is a companion page to Page 5. Again, different students will use different methods to find the solutions. Some will draw the line of symmetry for the design on the left and then will look for the correct "half" with the correct fold line location. Others will look for each "half" piece within the original design making sure there is the proper symmetry. Others may want to use a mirror to complete "halves". Still others may wish to use their hands or a piece of paper to block off "half" of the original design. It is fun to compare and share the numerous methods used.

Discussing what is wrong with the incorrect responses not only helps students to see subtle visual distinctions but also to verbalize their visual findings. Such

discussions should be encouraged, but not b[...]

Examples of interesting things to notice abou[...] wrong responses:

1. A. left portion, but horizontal line of symmetry.
   B. should be rejected immediately as very dissimilar.
   C. right portion, but horizontal line of symmetry.
   E. wrong location of fold line.
2. A. bottom portion, but vertical line of symmetry.
   B. an exchange of curved and straight lines.
   C. an exchange of curved and straight lines; also opposite point in lower right portion.
   D. top portion, but vertical line of symmetry.
3. A. opposite curvature.
   B. top portion, but vertical line of symmetry.
   D. bottom portion, but vertical line of symmetry.
   E. wrong location of fold line.
4. A. opposite curvatures.
   B. right portion, but horizontal line of symmetry.
   C. wrong location of fold line.
   E. left portion, but horizontal line of symmetry.
5. A. right portion, but horizontal line of symmetry.
   C. left portion, but horizontal line of symmetry.
   D. opposite curvatures.
   E. opposite curvatures.

Page 7:

1. I   2. F   3. E   4. A   5. H   6. C   7. D   8. B   9. J   10. G

Students enjoy the self-checking aspect of this page, as there is a one-to-one correspondence between designs and folded pieces. When they finish this page, there is a sense of completeness and closure.

As with any matching exercise, some students will work sequentially; while others will skip around. Crossing out or checking off what has already been matched will help students organize their work and stay focused.

Some students will match the pieces at the bottom of the page to the designs at the top of the page; while others will draw the lines of symmetry for the designs at the top of the page and will look for those "halves" at the bottom of the page. Observing students' learning styles with these spatial exercises is interesting and informative.

Page 8:

1. G   2. E   3. A   4. J   5. B   6. I   7. C   8. F   9. H   10. D

This is a companion page to Page 7. The same comments apply.

Page 9:

1. D   2. none   3. B, C, E   4. C, E   5. A, B, D

This is the first time that there is the possibility of multiple answers or no answer. The way that more than two answers is possible is to start with a design that has both a horizontal and a vertical line of symmetry, such as in examples 3 and 5.

udents have only partial answers, encourage to find all of them by telling them how many swers there are.

Again students should be encouraged to discuss what is wrong with the incorrect responses.

Page 10:

1. A, B, C, E	2. none	3. A, B, E
4. B, E	5. B, D, E	

This is a companion page to Page 9. The number of possible correct responses ranges from 0 to 4. More than two responses are possible when the original design has both a horizontal and a vertical line of symmetry, such as in examples 1, 3, 4, and 5. However, in example 4, only two of the four possibilities are given.

Pages 11-20: General Comments

Pages 11-20 are devoted to parts-to-whole problems. Students are presented with a "piece" that has been cut from a folded sheet of paper with the fold line indicated. They then have to find the "whole" design that would result from unfolding the cut-out piece. In these activities, internal details have been added to the designs. These internal cut-outs indeed have to be taken into consideration in determining what the unfolded design will be!

Some students view the internal details as confusing distractions. Other students latch onto them as important salient features helpful to the decision making process.

If these activities are not as well-liked by some students, they are not hindered from jumping ahead to the next whole-to-parts section starting on Page 21, which parallels Pages 1-10 but uses two fold lines instead of one. In other words, Pages 21-30 could precede Pages 11-20. However, Pages 11-20 need to precede Pages 31-40.

It should be noted that the pieces in Pages 11-20 are not pictured with the border of the paper showing since they are viewed as actual cut-outs, not pieces to be cut out. Again the fold line is indicated by a dotted line.

Page 11:

1. C	2. D	3. E	4. B

Again, students will approach these problems in a variety of ways. Some will conceive in their minds of unfolding the piece. Others will look for the "half" as part of the "whole" with the fold line in the proper place. Others will look for a line of symmetry in the designs on the right and immediately rule out any design that doesn't have a line of symmetry. For those designs that do have a line of symmetry, they may dot it in and then compare the "half" with the given piece.

It is useful to discuss why the incorrect choices are wrong. For example:

1. A. This would be correct if the fold line were at the bottom of the piece rather than the top.

B. There is no line of symmetry; hence this can't be an unfolded design for anything.
D. There is no line of symmetry.
E. Even though there is a horizontal line of symmetry, the shape is not correct.

A similar discussion should take place for the other problems. This discussion should be kept light, fun, and investigative. Don't belabor the issues so that the enthusiasm gets dampened. Some of the discrepancies in the designs are very subtle, such as 2A where only one small line has been changed from curved to straight, or 4E where the internal rectangles are not in the correct location. Let the students liken themselves to detectives!

Page 12:

1. E	2. C	3. E	4. A

Page 12 is a companion page to Page 11. The same comments apply.

Page 13:

1. H 2. D 3. I 4. B 5. G 6. E 7. J 8. C 9. A 10. F

Students enjoy the self-checking nature of this page, as there is a one-to-one correspondence between pieces at the top of the page and unfolded designs at the bottom of the page. When they finish this page, there is a sense of completeness and closure.

Some students will do the matching exercises sequentially, while others will skip around. Crossing out or checking off what has already been matched will help students organize their work and stay focused.

Some students will match the pieces at the top of the page with the designs at the bottom of the page. Others will draw the line of symmetry for each design at the bottom of the page and look for that "half" at the top of the page.

Some students will rely more on the outside shape rather than the internal detail. Others will focus more heavily on the relative placements of the internal detail. Whichever way students do the problems is fine and a matter of preferred style. They then can be encouraged to use the other way as a check.

Page 14:

1. F 2. H 3. A 4. J 5. C 6. I 7. D 8. G 9. B 10. E

Page 14 is a companion page to Page 13. The same comments apply.

Page 15:

1. C	2. none	3. E	4. D

Page 15 is similar to Pages 11 and 12 except that there may be one answer or no answer and there is greater complexity in the internal details. The comments given for Page 11 apply here.

Page 16:

1. D	2. D	3. E	4. none

Page 16 is similar to Page 15. The comments for Pages 15 and 11 apply here.

Page 17:

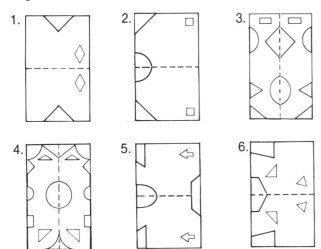

Students are asked to draw the design they would get if they unfolded each of the given pieces on the dotted line. Some students will welcome drawing these designs; while others may find it difficult. Drawings do not need to be absolutely precise.

Students may wish to use mirrors to help them. If students do enjoy drawing designs given the "half" pieces, they may wish to redo Pages 7, 8, 13, and 14 with the task to complete the designs and then to check their drawings with the completed designs pictured on the other portion of the page.

Page 18:

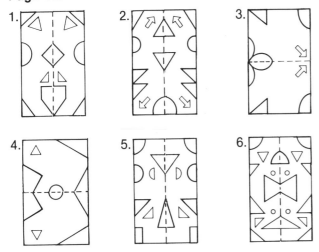

Page 18 is a companion to Page 17. The same comments apply.

Page 19:

A and L	B and H	C and M	D and I
E and K	F and N	G and O	J and P

Students are asked to match pairs of pieces that would give the same design if they unfolded each on the dotted line. Some matches are relatively easy, as a left portion and right portion match, or a top portion and a bottom portion match. However, for designs that actually have two lines of symmetry, students may be asked to match a horizontal piece with a vertical piece, A and L.

It is interesting to note that whenever the design h two lines of symmetry, indeed the piece also has a lin of symmetry. A case where this does not happen would be C. With this insight, you would know that the match of C has to be the "top half". However, even if the piece has a line of symmetry, as in the case of G, the match could still be the "other half" like O.

As can be seen from the above comments, these pages lend themselves to interesting discussions. The value comes from talking out these issues, not just doing the problems.

Every piece on the page has exactly one match, so this sheet brings a comforting sense of completeness and closure to students.

Page 20:

A and O	B and I	C and F	D and L
E and N	G and J	H and M	K and P

Page 20 is a companion to Page 19. The same comments apply.

Pages 21-30: General Comments

Pages 21-30 parallel Pages 1-10, but use two fold lines and "quarters", rather than one fold line and "halves". They could follow Page 10 directly and may be easier for some students who prefer whole-to-parts reasoning than Pages 11-20, which focus on parts-to-whole reasoning (with a possible overload of internal details). It is possible and even desirable for some students to do Pages 21-30 prior to Pages 11-20.

Even though some of the designs seen previously had two lines of symmetry, all of the pieces used have been "halves". Now both lines of symmetry will be used at the same time. Designs will be cut from doubly folded paper using "quarters". The fold lines will again be dotted in.

Pages 21-23 explore figures with two lines of symmetry. Students would benefit from actually cutting their own designs from doubly folded paper as an introductory exercise.

The exercises on Pages 24-30 are carefully sequenced. Extensive comments are given for each of the pages to help provide a rich spatial experience for students.

Page 21:

1. 1	2. 0	3. 2	4. 1
5. 0	6. 2	7. 2	8. 0

Even though only the number of lines of symmetry are reported above in the answers, students should have drawn on their page the lines of symmetry using dotted lines. In exercise 1, the single line of symmetry is horizontal; in exercise 4, it is vertical.

Students should be encouraged to check their answers by cutting out the figures and folding on the dotted

 Spatial Problem Solving with Paper Folding and Cutting © 1984 Cuisenaire Co. of America, Inc.

especially important in the case of two lines
[sym]metry for them to note that it does not matter
[whic]h of the lines they fold on first.

Page 22:

1. 1   2. 2   3. 0   4. 2   5. 1   6. 0
7. 2   8. 2   9. 0   10. 1   11. 1   12. 2

Page 22 practices the ideas of Page 21. The same comments apply.

Page 23:

1. C   2. E

Page 23 is a teaching page to show how to cut a design from doubly folded paper. The focus should be on the four possible ways to do this. It is possible to use the "upper left quarter", "upper right quarter", "lower left quarter", or "lower right quarter". Note the importance of the locations of the two fold lines shown by dotted lines.

Page 24:

1. D   2. B   3. C   4. E   5. A

Page 24 is similar to Page 5 except for its dealing with two fold lines rather than one. Each design in the left hand column can be cut from a doubly folded piece pictured in the right hand column. Students have to find the correct piece. In doing so, some students will dot in the two lines of symmetry and then will look for the correct "quarter" with the correct fold line location. Others may look for the piece within the whole design in the proper location.

It is very constructive, after the correct answers have been found, to discuss why the other choices for answers are incorrect. This type of discussion enriches the spatial problem solving experience.

Examples of interesting and subtle things to notice about the wrong responses include:
- an exchange of curved and straight lines
- opposite curvatures
- combinations of both situations

Page 25:

1. C   2. A   3. D   4. C   5. D

Page 25 is a companion page to Page 24. The same comments apply.

Page 26:

1. C, E   2. B, C, E   3. none   4. D   5. A, B, D, E

This page introduces the possibility of 0, 1, 2, 3, or 4 correct answers. Students need to concentrate on the locations of the double fold lines.

Again, students should be encouraged to discuss the incorrect choices.

Page 27:

1. C 2. F 3. J 4. G 5. E 6. H 7. I 8. B 9. A 10. D

Students enjoy the self-checking aspect of this page,

as there is a one-to-one correspondence between designs and doubly folded pieces. When they finish this page, there is a sense of completeness and closure.

As with any matching exercises, some students will work sequentially; while others will skip around. Students should check off what has already been matched to help them organize their work.

Some students will match the pieces at the bottom of the page to the designs at the top of the page; while others will draw in the two lines of symmetry at the top of the page and will look for those "quarters" at the bottom of the page. The position of the two fold lines is very vital.

Page 28:

1. D 2. F 3. E 4. J 5. A 6. I 7. C 8. G 9. H 10. B

Page 28 is a companion page to Page 27. The same comments apply.

Page 29:

1. B, D   2. A, C, D   3. none   4. D   5. A, C, D, E

Page 29 is very similar to page 26, but no clues are given as to the position of the piece. Greater focus needs to be placed on the two fold lines.

The number of possible correct answers ranges from 0-4. Students again should discuss the subtleties of the incorrect options.

Page 30

1. C, D, E   2. A, B, D, E   3. C, D   4. none   5. B

Page 30 is a companion page to Page 29. The same comments apply.

Pages 31-40: General Comments

Pages 31-40 cover parts-to-whole relationships with two fold lines and should be preceded by Pages 11-20 which deal with parts-to-whole relationships with one fold line. Students are presented with a piece that has been cut from a doubly folded sheet of paper with the two fold lines indicated. They then have to find the "whole" design that would result from unfolding the cut-out piece. The pieces have internal details which have also been cut out, and these interior parts also have to be taken into consideration in determining what the unfolded design will be.

Some students view the internal details as confusing distractions which they prefer to deal with last in the decision making process. Other students latch onto them as important salient features which they focus on first to narrow down the choices and rule out possibilities. The different styles with which students solve these problems should be discussed and shared to enhance the richness of the experience.

Page 31:

1. D   2. C   3. B   4. E

Students are asked to find the design in the right hand

column that will result from unfolding the doubly folded piece in the left hand column. Again, students will approach these problems in a variety of ways. Some will conceive in their minds of unfolding the piece vertically and then horizontally. Others will conceive in their minds of unfolding the piece horizontally and then vertically. (It doesn't matter which is done first!) Other students will look for the "quarter" piece as part of the "whole" with the fold lines in the proper places. Others will look for the two lines of symmetry in the design on the right and perhaps will draw them in so that they can compare the "quarter" of the design with the given piece. (If any of the designs do not have two lines of symmetry, they can be eliminated immediately from being a possible answer.)

It is useful to discuss why the incorrect choices are wrong. In some cases it will be a problem with the external border, and in other cases with the internal details, or even both.

Students may wish to fold paper and cut out designs similar to the ones shown in the left hand column. Actually unfolding to find the results may be more convincing as to what happens when there are two fold lines and internal details than simply drawing the two lines of symmetry on the designs pictured in the right hand column.

Page 32:

1. B   2. D   3. C   4. E

Page 32 is a companion page to Page 31. The same comments apply.

Page 33:

1. I 2. D 3. G 4. E 5. B 6. C 7. J 8. A 9. H 10. F

Students enjoy the self-checking aspect of this matching exercise. Some students will do the matching process sequentially; while others will skip around. Crossing out or checking off what has already been matched will help students organize their work.

Some students will match the pieces at the top of the page with the designs at the bottom of the page. Others will draw the lines of symmetry for each design at the bottom of the page and will look for that "quarter" at the top of the page.

Some students will focus more on external borders in the decision making process and use the internal detail as a check. Others will use the placement of the internal details as their primary concern.

Page 34:

1. E 2. H 3. B 4. I 5. D 6. C 7. J 8. F 9. A 10. G

Page 34 is a companion page to Page 33. The same comments apply.

Page 35:

1. D   2. none   3. B   4. C

Page 35 is similar to Pages 31 and 32 except that there

may be one answer or no answer. The comments for Page 31 apply here.

Page 36:

1. none   2. C   3. B   4. none

Page 36 is similar to Page 35. The comments for Pages 35 and 31 apply here.

Page 37:

Students are asked to draw the design they would get if they unfolded each of the given pieces on the two dotted fold lines. One way to do this is to draw the given piece in the proper quadrant and then to consider one line of symmetry at a time. Some students like to use mirrors to help them. The drawings do not need to be absolutely precise for a student who finds this activity difficult. Some students love drawing unfolded designs and may wish to go back to Pages 33 and 34 to draw those as well.

Page 38:

a companion page to Page 37. The same
its apply.

39:

and L	B and M	C and F	D and K
E and O	G and I	H and N	J and P

Students enjoy the self-checking aspect of this
matching exercise. Some students will proceed
sequentially; while others will skip around. Crossing
out or checking off what has already been matched will
help students keep track of their work.

Some students will benefit from cutting these designs
out of doubly folded paper and checking the matches
concretely. The placement of the two fold lines indicated by the dotted lines is critical. The cut-out
designs could be used as a bulletin board display.

Page 40:

A and K	B and P	C and I	D and N
E and O	F and L	G and M	H and J

Page 40 is a companion page to Page 39. The same
comments apply.

Pages 41-44: General Comments

Pages 41-44 extend the ideas to three fold lines.
Anyone who is following just the whole-to-parts se-
quence in this book would do pages 1-10 with one fold
line, pages 21-30 with two fold lines, and now possibly
pages 41-44 with three fold lines. Dealing with three
fold lines is much more challenging to visualize than
one or two folds. This section should be done only with
students who are eager and ready to take it on.

A great deal of work should be done with actual folding
and cutting experience. Students should observe the
one horizontal line of symmetry in the unfolded figure.
Then they should observe the one vertical line of symmetry in the unfolded figure. What is subtle and interesting is that the "top half" has its own horizontal
line of symmetry; and the "bottom half" has its own
horizontal line of symmetry. If all of these "lines of
symmetry" are drawn, the figure is divided into eight
congruent parts.

Page 41:

This is a teaching page intended to start off the work
on three fold lines. Students should become adept at
folding the paper, first horizontally, then vertically, then
horizontally. Of course, this is not the only way to triply
fold paper, but is the procedure which is used con-
sistently in this development.

In the folded piece of paper, only two fold lines show.
The convention is still to use dotted lines for the fold
lines. A new convention of placing a dot to indicate
where the four original corners of the paper are located
is introduced.

The ideas on this page will need to be reiterated and
reviewed constantly as the students work with the rest
of the book.

Page 42:

1. B	2. D	3. F	4. E	5. A	6. C

All of the designs at the top of the page can be cut from
a triply folded piece of paper. It would be desirable to
teach the students how you would know that from the
"lines of symmetry" of the design.

First, draw the horizontal line of symmetry. Then draw
the vertical line of symmetry. Then note that each of
the "quarter" pieces has a horizontal line of symmetry
(which is not a line of symmetry for the entire design).
Relate these "lines of symmetry" to the three fold lines
made in the original sheet of paper.

Note also that when all the "lines of symmetry" are
drawn, the design is split into eight congruent parts.

On this page, all of the pieces at the bottom of the page
are really the "eighth" piece that is at the bottom right
of the matching unfolded design at the top of the page.

Knowing all of this information about how the three
folds work makes these problems very easy to do
analytically. It is conceivable that some students will
do these problems mechanically and not visually ap-
preciate the spatial aspects. When this happens, have
them go back to folding the paper and cutting the sug-
gested pieces.

Page 43:

1. D	2. E	3. C	4. C	5. D

Page 43 is similar to Page 42. The same comments
apply. Since students have to deal here with possible
wrong choices, it is desirable to discuss why each
wrong choice will not produce the desired design.
Again students may wish to cut each of the pieces from
triply folded paper to see what the unfolded designs
look like. These are very easy to cut provided you
observe carefully the two folded edges of the triply
folded paper (indicated by the two dotted lines) and the
corner where the four original corners of the paper are
located (indicated by the dot).

Page 44:

1. C, D	2. A	3. none	4. D, E	5. B, D, E

Page 44 is very similar to Pages 42 and 43. The same
comments apply. However, in this case, there may be
none, one, or more than one correct answer. There is a
greater need to consider each piece pictured in the
right hand column. If students do not find all the
answers at first, tell them how many there are and let
them continue the search.

Pages 45-48: General Comments

Pages 45-48 should be done only if Pages 41-44 were
well understood by a student. These pages do the
parts-to-whole relationships with three folds.

Page 45:

1. D	2. B	3. D	4. D

It is helpful for some students to draw the lines of symmetry for each design in the right hand column. First,

draw the horizontal line of symmetry. Then draw the vertical line of symmetry. Then note that each of the "quarter" pieces has a horizontal line of symmetry (which is not a line of symmetry for the entire design). When all the "lines of symmetry" are drawn, the design is split into eight congruent parts. Then it is just a matter of finding which of the little pieces in its proper location matches the given piece. (Of course, if a design does not have the proper symmetry, it can be ruled out, for example 1B.)

Other students will immediately find the piece within the unfolded design. In this exercise, all of the pieces are located in the lower right hand corner, as indicated by the fold lines and dot.

Page 46:

1. C   2. A   3. E   4. D

Page 46 is an extension of Page 45. Here the pieces are located in a variety of positions, as indicated by the fold lines and dots. Some students will immediately find the piece within the unfolded design. Other students will wish to draw the "lines of symmetry" for each of the designs in the right hand column.

Page 47:

 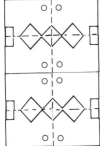  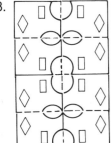 

Students are asked to draw what they would get if they unfolded each of the given triply folded pieces. They are best to draw the given piece in the lower right hand corner, as indicated by the fold lines and dot; and then use the lines of symmetry to complete the figure step-by-step. The drawings do not need to be absolutely precise.

Page 48:

Here the given pieces are in a variety of locations: 1) top left 2) top right 3) bottom left 4) bottom right.

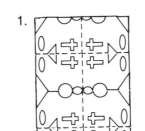 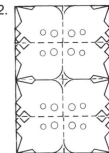 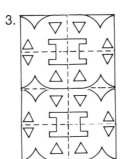 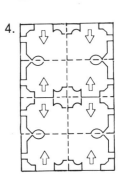

Students should draw the given piece in the proper location and then use the lines of symmetry to complete the figure step-by-step. The drawings do not need to be absolutely precise.

Pages 49-50: General Comments

These two pages introduce changes in orientation by rotation and/or reflection. This section should be done only by students who have experienced the earlier sections with a great deal of success.

Page 49:

More than one description of the change in orientation is possible for each piece. Only one possible description is given here.

1B. One horizontal fold line.
    Top "half" reflected.
1C. One horizontal fold line.
    Top "half" rotated.
2A. Two fold lines.
    Top right "quarter" rotated.
2B. One horizontal fold line.
    Top "half" rotated.
2C. Two fold lines.
    Bottom left "quarter" rotated.
3A. One horizontal fold line.
    Bottom "half" rotated.
3B. Three fold lines.
    Upper right "eighth" rotated.
3C Two fold lines.
    Top right "quarter" rotated.

This page is essential as a discussion page for the upcoming work on Pages 50-53. Students enjoy talking about the changes in orientation more than writing about them.